ISAIAH

Also by Daniel Berrigan

Prose

The Bride; Essays in the Church
The Bow in the Clouds
Consequences; Truth and
Love, Love at the End
They Call Us Dead Men
Night Flight to Hanoi
No Bars to Manhood
The Dark Night of Resistance
America is Hard to Find
The Geography of Faith (with Robert Coles)
Absurd Convictions, Modest Hopes (with Lee Lockwood)
Jesus Christ
Lights on in the House of the Dead
The Raft Is Not the Shore (with Thich Nhat Hanh)
A Book of Parables
Uncommon Prayer; A Book of Psalms
Beside the Sea of Glass; The Song of the Lamb
The Words our Savior Taught Us
The Discipline of the Mountain
We Die Before We Live
Portraits; Of Those I Love
Ten Commandments for the Long Haul
The Nightmare of God
Steadfastness of the Saints
The Mission
To Live in Peace: Autobiography
A Berrigan Reader
Stations (with Margaret Parker)
Sorrow Built a Bridge
Whereon to Stand (Acts of Apostles)
Minor Prophets, Major Themes

Poetry

Time Without Number
Encounters
The World for Wedding Ring
No One Walks Waters
False Gods, Real Men
Trial Poems (with Tom Lewis)
Prison Poems
Selected and New Poems
May All Creatures Live
Block Island
Jubilee
Tulips in the Prison Yard
Homage (to G.M. Hopkins)

Drama

The Trial of the Catonsville Nine

ISAIAH

Spirit of Courage,
Gift of Tears

Daniel Berrigan

FORTRESS PRESS

MINNEAPOLIS

ISAIAH
Spirit of Courage, Gift of Tears

Unless otherwise noted, the text of Isaiah is given here in modern equivalent by Daniel Berrigan.

The woodcut of Isaiah on the front cover, created for this book, and the woodcut of Daniel Berrigan on the back cover, are by Robert McGovern.

Cover and book design by Joseph Bonyata

Library of Congress Cataloging-in-Publication Data
Berrigan, Daniel
        Isaiah : spirit of courage, gift of tears / Daniel Berrigan.
            p.   cm.
        Includes bibliographical references.
        ISBN 0-8006-2998-1 (alk. paper)
            1. Bible. O. T. Isaiah—Criticism, interpretation, etc.
I. Title.
BS1515.2B47 1996
224'.106—dc20   96-18021
                                                                              CIP

The paper used in this publication meets the minimum requirements of American National Standard for Information Sciences—Permanence of Paper for Printed Library Materials, ANSI Z329.48-1984.

Manufactured in the U.S.A.   AF 1-2998
01   00   99   98   97   2   3   4   5   6   7   8   9   10

William Hart McNichols, S.J.

your life

our icon

Contents

Introduction

Over against those who would separate the pastoral from the prophetic, I offer here an exercise in pastoral prophecy. Isaiah and his school would have us read aright the signs of the times and, in the light thus gained, would urge us to render judgment on the times. The prophetic-pastoral concern permeates the book of Isaiah with moral clear-sightedness and courage under the threat of disaster.

The reflections in this book had a long incubation. From coast to coast in the United States and in Europe and Australia, in retreats, lectures, and university courses, the passion and tenderness and tears and thunders and clairvoyance of the heart of Isaiah beat on and on.

The ultimate beginnings of this book can be traced to a group of homeless folk in New York City who were offered a weekend of retreat and relief away from life on the mean streets. Nuns north of the city invited us to the peace and plenty of their retreat house. On arrival we inquired of our guests, "What shall we reflect on?"

They answered, "The Bible."

"And what part of the Bible?"

"Isaiah," they said.

"Why Isaiah?"

"He speaks about justice!"

For seventeen years our community, called Kairos ("the right time") has hung together, joined with others of like mind in the vast sprawl of urban misery, keeping at something that has been known for a generation as the "peace movement." We have vigiled, fasted, leafleted, and been arrested—again and again. Our middle name is trouble; our ambit is the courtroom.

The scene of the crime might be midtown Manhattan, the lair of the Riverside Research Institute, an entity much like its Pentagon parent, at once notorious and anonymous, fatly funded, aloof and snooty and sterilized and beyond accountability in its elegant art deco aerie. Day after day and year after year, a squad of spoiled darlings of the culture, the highly seeded scientists and engineers, conspire above an endless menu of nuclear and "conventional" goodies. To enter their workplace, they must step over or around the recumbent bodies of the homeless along West Forty-second and Forty-third streets. At their comings and goings the upstarts stand or sit or leaflet, saying to them, "Thanks, but no thanks."

Isaiah is familiar with conflict; Isaiah's faith is defined by conflict, crisis, the clash between the principalities and ourselves.

From Isaiah's time to ours and in every year in between, there has been war—a continuum of war with the swagger and braggadocio of the powers of death, declaring themselves the molders of human fate, the givers of all good. In their wake is a procession of slaves and loot—and the dead.

But then emerges something else, a far different vision of who we are and where we are bound. Isaiah appears with his great refusal, with clarity, courage and no kowtowing. Isaiah set his face against the feverish vacillations of the king and his bogus court prophets. Isaiah would have nothing of the war then occurring or any other. Let the king take note; God would have none of it. It was thunderous and steady, his word. But his word went unheeded. Pacts with "the nations" were concluded, and war broke out.

How, in such a world, could the word of God survive? That it did survive was astonishing, utterly beyond explanation. Could the miracle be traced to Isaiah himself? to his integrity and courage, to the fact that he lived the word, endured it, and paid for it? The word before all else had to pass through his being.

It was in the summer of 1980 that our group discovered—or

was discovered by—the book of Isaiah. It seemed at the time that we had all accidentally broken the crust of a cave and come on a treasure in a stone jar. The prophet had been there all the time, but now he was *our* Isaiah.

That summer we met frequently, friends seeking in Scripture a metaphor or an image that would shed light upon the question that haunted us: What were we to do in face of the mad proliferation of nuclear weapons? We sweated and struggled. Finally a light dawned, lit by Molly Rush, mother and grandmother, founder and soul of the Thomas Merton Center in Pittsburgh. She suggested a text, we opened our Bibles, and soon life was turned on its head;

> God will judge the nations.
> They will beat their swords into plowshares,
> their spears into pruning knives.
>
> (Isaiah 2:4)

We took our small household hammers (and our smaller courage) and, on September 9, 1980, entered the General Electric Reentry Division plant in King of Prussia, Pennsylvania. There, in a sprawl of nondescript warehouses, the Mark 12 A missile, a first-strike nuclear horror, had been put together for shipping to Amarillo, Texas, for its payload—a technological doomsday. There it squatted, the General Electric factory, with bombs its secret, its workers sworn to secrecy. We walked into a terra incognita known as the geography of faith, a terrain by turns icy and torrid, in which Isaiah also had stood. Others since the prophet have stood there, a "cloud of witnesses" who found in the biblical word the resources to go on.

Isaiah, as we have come to know, lived in a time astonishingly like ours—with war and rumors of war. In the great prophetic tradition, he intervened directly in political, military, and diplomatic events. For a time, he was an oracular presence at court, honored and hearkened to by the high and mighty. Then he predicted the invasion of his country; it happened twice. He lived to see his beloved Jerusalem besieged. In all this, royal sensibilities were offended.

Then Isaiah donned the garb of a court fool—one who mimes foolishness in high places. At first, he survived. Finally he was cast out. Far from being broken, his spirit seemed transfigured. He began to play hound of heaven, raising very hell at the wheels of the imperial chariots. He died, tradition tells, under those wheels.

Yet Isaiah's word was not entirely nor finally defeated. Others, some of his time and some of the next generation, heard and obeyed. They were a minority, a kind of base community who passed on the word. The early oracles were amended, collated, added to. An "Isaian" school arose.

In this book I comment on certain of the crucial passages from Isaiah, using my own translation. In reading these portions one may reflect on Isaiah's prophecies against Judah, his call to be a prophet, his visions that carry the hope of the child named Emmanuel, his word of judgment and hope regarding the nations, and his portrayal of the faithful servant of God.

Isaiah lived in a time of whetted swords and rusted plowshares, of immense violence and social conflict and neglect of the poor. Then the oracle came to him—swords into plowshares! What does Isaiah have to say to us?

1
The Winnowing Time—
The Nation under Judgment

The book of Isaiah begins with a "vision" that he "saw," not a word that he heard. But the vision is translated, transmitted, in words. Moral instruction that follows grows out of the vision. Such, according to the prophets, is the only morality worth talking about or taking seriously. The implication is inescapable; the prophet has seen the vision, the hope of God for our humankind.

What might be the moral conduct of those who have seen and been led by a vision, who strive to care for the widow and orphan, the homeless, the refugees, and the war veterans in our midst? Such tasks require sure vision, one that is constantly renewed, a vision of God who instructs us in godly behavior.

This People, Rebellious from Birth (1:1–9)

1:1   The vision of Isaiah son of Amoz concerning Judah and Jerusalem, which he saw in the reign of Uzziah, Jotham, Ahaz, and Hezekiah, kings of Judah.

2   Heaven and earth I call to witness—
this people
so favored, so cosseted—
rebellious from birth!

3   The ox knows its drover,
    the ass its stall—
    my own turn aside, dishonor me.
4   Evildoers, bloodline
    tainted with crime,
    sons perverted, betraying—
    turn about is fair! Ruin awaits!

    . . . .

6   Sole of foot to head's crown
    no health. Rot, infestation,
    suppurating wound.

7   I see, I lament—
    the land a desert, the cities
    afire, foreigners ravaging.

    . . . .

9   Had not a remnant survived—
    pure catastrophe!
    Sodom, Gomorrah—you!

The sequence of vision followed by ethic is hardly honored in society then or now. The behavior of "this people" is wildly amiss. Isaiah begins with a disturbing report from Yahweh, a situation apparent to all except the people involved. Deprived of the vision that had been granted their prophet, the people grew wicked.

Thus, the atmosphere of the book of Isaiah from the beginning is heavy with foreboding. The word of God must strike against a world that provokes contrasting moods. The underlying motif is obvious: The word that God offers us, whether of wisdom or celebration or consolation or rebuke or judgment, inevitably foreshadows or follows a war.

Is this "vision" to be linked with Isaiah's temple vision in chapter 6? If so, it must be interpreted in transcendent terms. We cannot assume that the sequence of the oracles reflects the historical sequence. But whatever form the vision took, whether the great chariot of Ezekiel or the burning bush of Moses, something of tremendous import to humanity follows. God is involved with us. Through the prophets God announces an ethical code to mortals.

This code delineates the form of the human in the shape of ideal, practical, robust, visionary, and self-giving ideals.

The people, then and now, are helpless to arrive at a godly ideal. Their religious, political, and cultural resources, assembled from various icons, heroes, saints, ancestors, warriors, kings, or priests, fall short. How can virtuous people deal with each other? How can they construct prohuman social, economic, religious, and political systems? Can they imagine a prohuman military system, or is this term itself an oxymoron?

Isaiah displays fury also against temple religion. His vision has not been granted the approval of the conventional religious establishment. The established religion, deprived of a vision, cannot embody or foster truly human behavior. It continues to function and even to prosper, but it presents dead relics of vision or the remnant of tradition or rite or even Scripture.

Such an establishment might reflect a strict sexual morality at the same time it is implicitly lax on public violence, especially toward war and the military state. The North American Roman Catholic bishops debated for more than a decade the morality of nuclear deterrence. It finally became obvious that they were so divided as a teaching body that they were unable to offer a clear message on the threat of mass murder.

"My own turn aside" (vv. 2 and 3). Even certain forms of worship become a positive impediment against true knowledge. "The ox knows its drover, the ass its stall," but "my people" know not even that. Beasts require no more than hunger to respond, but what do such a people require that they might respond to God and to one another? Knowledge has been denied them, knowledge that casts a light on God and the human family, honors the covenant, and makes for a livable world. But the people have fallen below the level of instinctual life. Animals have no prophets, but they are a measure against which the prophets may affirm or criticize the quality of our lives.

Isaiah is reticent in matters concerning himself. His moral code, like the details of his vision, must be inferred. If the people know nothing, Isaiah must know something. He knows, at the least, that the people, including the religious system, "know nothing."

The pronouncement of verse 2, seemingly banal, is a great event, a disruption in nature. The heavens have opened, and a source of knowledge has been granted a mortal. This knowledge leads to a devastating critique. For all your pretensions and dreams of grandeur, for all public evidence of your greatness, you know nothing.

Where are the Isaiahs of our day? Could they be found among the outsiders—a prisoner or a widow or an orphan or a homeless one or an "illegal alien" or someone driven mad by the system? The vision often starts among such persons who can cut to the essentials in matters of life and death, of compassion and right judgment, while the rest of us know nothing.

There is, however, a note of compassion. It is my people who are ignorant. This note will be sounded repeatedly in later chapters of the book of Isaiah.

This phrase is rich in self-contradiction. Not everyone knows nothing. Someone knows that everyone knows nothing, and someone says so. Then a few who hear the audacious judgment agree with it and pass it on. The statement is set down. Generations read and ponder it and pray to be delivered from it. An iron circle is thereby broken.

Verses 4–9 describe the consequence of such blindness as has been declared in verses 2 and 3. Isaiah's words speak of the collective plight, fullness of sin from "sole of foot to head's crown." Some precious thing is being weighed in the balance; it is then traded, handed over, for gain. In the final analysis we betray and hand over our own humanity, deprived of soundness.

Isaiah's imagery reminds us of a colony of lepers, untended, physically ravaged, and demoralized. The entire social body is involved, "from the sole of foot to head's crown"; nothing remains sound. There are only bruises, welts, and raw wounds.

Each stricken one is abandoned by others who themselves are abandoned. Each is left to a horrid fate of loneliness and despair. All are deprived of saving compassion, all equally afflicted. There could be no more awful image of the "Fall" as it strikes down cultural optimism, the myth of progress, the claim of humanity coming of age, and the many forms of religious self-justification.

The verses that follow repeat a recurrent emphasis in the Bible: our sinful estate does not stop with ourselves. Sinfulness fills the sinful community, brims over into the living beings of nature with afflictions, insults, and pollution.

"The land a desert, the cities afire . . ." (v. 7). Isaiah's vision lingers over the results of our malice. We, the defendants, do not stand apart in the docket; the judgment afflicts the world and leads to a ravaged creation. Countryside and the city are afflicted with blight. Jerusalem, the golden city, is reduced to a jerry-built hut or it is under siege, the siege of sin, injustice, and vain worship, which are the enemy within the gates.

The accusations form a widening circle until the desolation reaches nature itself. The verdict is certain: guilty.

Yet a glimmer of light appears amid the miasma of darkness. A great boulder is rolled away from the mouth of a tomb. It is "a remnant" (v. 9), a resurrection; it is Isaiah himself, and any and every saving exception to the awful rule of death. The Isaiahs of this world are those who deny hegemony to the empire of death, even at the cost of valiant lives.

True Worship? Seek Justice! (1:10–20)

1:10 Hear my voice!

11 Of what import, what value
these sacrifices of yours,
innumerable—useless, repugnant!

12 Why to and fro, processions
witless about the temple?

13 The smoke of your incense
stinks in my nostrils!

14 New moon or waning, Sabbath,
pilgrimage—
I hate with all my being!

15 Your prayer wheels hum and whir
in vagrant winds.
You stretch your arms to me,
I turn aside in disgust—
your hands reeking of blood.

. . . .

17   Turn, turn, turn!
      Seek justice,
      succor the oppressed,
      cherish the defenseless!

18   Then come, be reconciled!
      If your sins are as scarlet
      they shall be blanched as snow.
19   Obey me, my creation
      fills you to overflowing, ecstatic;
20   Defy, a sword
      I swear
      will lodge in your throat.

This diatribe, like other early oracles of Isaiah, reminds us of Amos (see Amos 5:21–24).

Unrelentingly, the rituals of Israel's worship are condemned. The conclusion is inescapable: It is the religious sense that is declared perverted. Such ritual refuses to rise heavenward, it lingers like damp smoke about the sanctuary, far from the truth of God. Equally lamentably, it has no role in judging public behavior, including that of the priesthood and the congregation. The justice of God has fled the land; there is no compassion, no care.

But just as despair is the ignoble stock-in-trade of the world's systems, hope is the noble stock-in-trade of the prophet. For "my people" some breakthrough, a personal and social change of heart is possible. The prophet is compelled to state this possibility and also to show a path.

Isaiah exhorts and threatens—a brimstone mix—but this is skillfully laved in tenderness (vv. 16–20). More accurately, Isaiah all but disappears, and Yahweh becomes the interlocutor. The initiative, the urgency, the love, and the word of truth are all a fire in the heart of Yahweh.

There is a whiplash at the end of this oracle, set down in the typical doublets of Hebrew poetry:

> If you consent and obey me
>> you will eat the fatness of the land.
> If you obstinately hold your present course,
>> it is the sword you will swallow.
>
> (1:19–20)

Isaiah's opponents, these eminences who promote temple religion with its offerings, moons, Sabbaths, assemblies, pilgrimages, and prayers, eat of the fat of the land. They offer no serious moral guidance, yet they are not forced to swallow a sword. Why this absurd image?

Secularized authorities are addressed in this oracle. They are skilled in war making and personal survival. They are unreconciled and obstinate. Their sins are as scarlet, red as their swords. That is the true definition and plight of those who enter the "system" and rise to become its authority. They and their system seem to prosper, but the sword will have the last word.

My Day Will Dawn: Swords into Plowshares (2:1–5)

2:1 The word that Isaiah son of Amoz saw concerning Judah and Jerusalem.

> 2 Behold my mountain
>> touching high heaven,
>> the temple of God crowning all!
> In that place,
>> the nations shall converge
> 3 crying:
>> "Come join with us
>> that Yahweh may teach us godly ways
>> as we walk in his paths!"

> 4 In that day, Arbiter over all,
>> God will judge the nations.
>> They will beat their swords into plowshares,
>> their spears into pruning knives.
>> Nevermore war

never again!
5   "Come, let us walk
in the light of Yahweh!"

"They will beat their swords into plowshares" (v. 4). For most of us, there exist one or two commanding texts, words that beckon us from "the paralysis of analysis," as Martin Luther King, Jr., would say, that beckon us toward simply "doing it" (Kierkegaard). To the Plowshares community, this text of Isaiah has been a summons—a vigorous word, a word that sets the human in motion.

The congruence of the times of Isaiah with our own times is striking, even unsettling. Isaiah lived in the eighth century before the common era. It was an age of imperial darkness, of wars and rumors of wars, of duplicity and conniving in high places.

When Isaiah entered upon this scene of desolating power, his voice was heard in the corridors of power. A religious figure of towering stature, and the most political of the prophets, he refused to separate public responsibility from the voice of God within. He had seen God; therefore he had a message to deliver to king and people. With a fiery and dangerous simplicity, the promise and conclusion were forged into one. His was the simplicity of a saint or a madman. In either case, he shortly became unsettling to conventional religion and politics.

For a while Isaiah had access to the throne of Ahaz, then to his successor Hezekiah. Then war with Assyria broke out. It proceeded bloodily; its resolution was shaky. Shortly the war, like every war, proved to be no more than a prelude to further rattling of arms. There was no end in sight. A war, in short, is self-perpetuating. Blood will have blood, in perpetuum—the law of Cain.

The world was bent on war. The Isaian voice dwelt at length on the bad outcome inevitable to morally dubious enterprises. Oftener than some might think healthy, he derided the foolishness and inflation of royal ego. His scorn was hardly reserved for his own. Pointing to Egypt, he called the Pharaoh and his advisers (and by implication, all such eminences) no more than "drunks, reeling in their vomit"(Isa. 19:14).

To the Israelites, Isaiah declared, your first war is no more than a first act. You will presently be invaded, and the jewel of your desire, Samaria, will fall. So it happened, and even worse befell: eventually a siege was laid to Jerusalem by Sennacherib of Assyria.

In those terrible years the Isaian voice was something to be reckoned with. Across the world the imperial adventurers—Egyptian, Assyrian, Sumerian—felt the sting of his prophecy. One truth, no borders!

Isaiah, and those who live in his tradition, announce the impossible: "They will beat their swords into plowshares." The necessary must somehow be fused with the impossible. Something new, something beyond all effort or genius or ecstatic longing or even imagining, must come to be. This historically impossible must happen to the inconvertible, the imperium, to those obsessed with violence and arms and the misuse of resources and the wanton expending of lives.

The truth of this transformation oracle, "swords into plowshares," is absolutely crucial to the prospering of nations and cultures, to the survival of individuals, of children and the elderly and the ill. It is crucial to honor, to religious faith, to a civilized sense of the human—crucial to the fate of the earth.

But the oracle is also impossible of fulfillment. Who in the time of Isaiah, who at present, believes it could come to pass? After Vietnam, after Granada, Panama, Iraq, Bosnia—who believes? Indeed, who in the churches could be said to believe?

War, any war, erupts. Shortly thereafter the "moral theologians" enter and the just-war nonsense is dusted off. With a great spasm of casuistry, the war is forced and fitted to the Procrustean theory. Swords are vindicated again, even as they kill.

Yet the conclusion of Isaiah must be vindicated. Although every poll and prevailing authority and purveyor of conventional wisdom and the preachments of ecclesiastical warriors proclaim it to be radically impossible, the task of transformation is crucial.

Those who have worked hardily against the war-making state know well the impossibility of the task. More than forty years of cold-war impasse, successive American wars, wars without issue or end, have frozen the hearts and minds of political and religious leaders. Citizens and churchgoers are literally stuck where they stand.

And yet the word of Isaiah must come to pass: "They will beat their swords into plowshares." The words surpass the human even while they engage the human in its deepest longings, in the lives of saints and martyrs and mystics. The words commit, invite, command, exact vows, demand conversion—of hearts as well as swords.

Like a command echoing in the tomb of a Lazarus, the words beckon into light our insipidities, our acceptance of dumb fate, our rehearsals of death. You are not helpless, you are not objects of fate, you are not dead. Despair is to your shame. Come forth!

Further, do not imagine that some magic or other will beat the world's swords into plowshares. You yourselves must act, you whom the times have beaten—in spirit, imagination, humanity—into the form of death. The blade lies at your own throat. You taste before death the death named despair.

Disarm; take into account at long last the widows and orphans and the poor to whom the sword has brought such grief, whom the sword has cheated. It cannot be done, yet it must be done. If it is to be done, it must be done—by ourselves.

Perhaps most terrifying of all, the beating of swords into plowshares lies beyond the stated morality of conventional religion. The churches, with some few exceptions, balk and cavil and bow low before the imperial usurpation. Rather than calling the nation to judgment, the churches are loud with conniving silence. They pronounce a sorry blessing on the forging and wielding of swords—a blessing that is a curse.

Yet the oracle will not be silenced. It sounds in our ears with absolute assurance: "They will beat their swords into plowshares, their spears into pruning knives." To say "they" shall do this is to say "ourselves," in our lifetime, in this generation—no other. It is, literally and brutally, now or never.

The oracle proceeds, Isaiah implies, from the fidelity of God. It implies a promise kept—wars shall cease.

The outcome is irresistible. No human malevolence, no nation, not the most powerful imperium in the world's history—none of these separately or together can foil the word of God. The tone of Isaiah is absolute, assured. The promise is uttered by God, and God is faithful.

The text invites an image. A hand appears, then many hands. Hands of women and men and children, of farmers and laborers, writers and artists, ministers, students, of old and young, hands of pacifists and former warriors. All these hands can be symbolized by the hands of two among us. The first is a farmer-poet, reflective, an essayist who cultivates, nurtures, and cherishes—a lover of children and of all living things.

The other is a converted warrior. This veteran has undergone a change of heart. He has joined the peacemakers and cast his military medals to the four winds.

Now the hands of these two grasp small hammers. They are impelled by both trepidation and courage. They enter a forbidden area, yet they proceed. They come upon the weaponry, the bomber, the submarine, the launching pad, the naval vessel. They bring their hammers down with force. They dent the weapon or crack its shell, blunt its cruel edge, neutralize its dread.

More than this: in seeking to transform the object beyond its original purpose as an instrument of death and maiming and bloodletting, they are themselves transformed.

Let me speak out of my own experience. I grew up in a farming family. Each spring I stumbled along after the plow as my father turned the earth, one furrow upon another. A sense of new life, damp, permeating, haunted with presences, arose in the mild air, so welcome after a killing north-country winter. I imagined that giants of the earth were turning over in sleep just before awakening. Or I thought of the furrows as great coils of rope, weaving, binding all things in one; earth and season, furrow and family, the horse plodding along, the planting, the harvest to follow, my father and me. It was all one. The blade of the plow wove the garment of the world.

In that garden of innocence, I thought the whole world was like my world. Plowing the earth was the normal function of humans; the true odor of the earth was earthy, the damp of soil. How could it be otherwise? How could the earth reek of blood or brimstone?

I had much to learn.

Years later, my four brothers enlisted for war. The scene was awesome, for more reasons than one. It was a very reversal and mockery of original innocence and truth, a truth the plowboy was one day to find verified in the prophet Isaiah.

The war was cold as a blade laid against his face. In effect, the plows of our farm and of every farm in the land, were not abandoned to rust or rot. "Lend-lease" was the cry, a war cry. The plows were beaten into swords. Overnight, swords sprang up in the furrows. They were the first shoots of a harvest of blood.

Now the sword made all the difference. The sword took the measure of the human. It was the only measure. How did this or that one measure up? The sword "sized up" a person; it was his credential, proof of citizenship. More, it became for many the proof of authentic Christianity.

What of the swordless, the unarmed, and, worst of all, the disarmed, the refusers, the objectors of conscience? They were summarily dealt with, stigmatized as shirkers, deserters, draft dodgers. They were hounded, ostracized, jailed.

And what of that discarded plow? Here or there, in Europe or elsewhere, a plow, perhaps in the hands of an old man or a child, turned up the earth as usual; and more, it turned up corpses and land mines.

And what of my brothers, scattered across the globe? During the war, the nation conferred new titles on them. They were no longer farmers, steel workers, students. They were warriors.

For those years of war, the lives of my brothers took on a static beat, the beat of muffled drums—or of muffled hearts. Their lives, like their clothing, went from multiform to uniform. So did their minds, cowed and obedient. "For the duration" they were pledged to kill, or to support, protect, back up those who killed. And when required (it was required for millions like them across the world), they were pledged to die.

And what of that plowboy? He had become a seminarian in the Jesuit order, and so was exempted from the fate of his brothers. Nonetheless, the war touched him, even as it taught him, and harshly. It was a hard school, harder by far than his Jesuit discipline. The boy learned fast. The climate of the world was fast changing. He must survive as best he could in a climate of cruelty.

Never again a season for plowing, always the winter, the sword.

Life came to this. As long as swords were drawn, we humans lost our bearings. We went literally mad—whether one thought of tradition or covenant or vocation or simply a recognizably human behavior. The social fabric was torn; the war ended through abominable deeds, mass murder. Huge crimes were committed, covered up or revealed, but in any case justified.

The God I had been taught to reverence, in family, in church and school—God of peace, God the giver of life—this One, as I became more and more convinced, lent neither presence nor approval nor blessing on the awful course of the war—any war.

What to make of such a God as the Gospels revealed, a God passionate for reconciling and healing? What to make of that famous Sermon on the Mount (even with all its millennial watering-down)? My lifetime was to be a perpetual wartime; other gods—Mars or Vulcan or Jupiter—were claiming sovereignty in the world.

Thus it occurred to me that wars shed a kind of horrid light on the myth of genesis. Modern war, technologized, devastating to the earth and to humans indiscriminately, was for all that trumpeted as virtuous and just. Yet war in effect reenacted the murder of Abel by Cain. We were killing our brothers and sisters. Every war was newly and horridly original. The gods of war, so to speak, have pressed their advantage, sensing victory. Policy, economics, religion, have favored them, even urged them on.

They plowed the earth—with swords. Then they sowed the ground with dragons' teeth—nuclear warheads, bunkers, bombers, laboratories. There sprang up from the furrows, a new species of humans—nuclear warriors. This was the most appalling event of all. An unheard-of species was conceived in the womb of war. The mutation celebrated the universal sway of the gods of war.

Peace? The word was meaningless; they had never known a time of peace. Or perhaps the word signified an illusion, the dream of this or that savior long discredited. The events suggest that the ideal human, as canonized by a nuclear culture, is the warrior.

In such a world, the consensus as to what constitutes "the human" must be questioned, then rendered suspect, and finally declared extinct. We must become used to, accepting of, murder. The prohibition against murder must in practice be removed from the Decalogue; even the memory of such a commandment. And it goes without saying that the Sermon on the Mount must be reduced to a dead letter.

Thus, too, the equation of the human as believer in the God of peace, the human marked by compassion, the human in search of justice, the human whose passion is the making of peace, must be canceled. All such must be consigned to a dustbin or a museum shelf—relics really, quaint survivors, recessive qualities of quondam devotees of a lesser God. The survivors, like a quavering coterie of aged Shakers, would of course be tolerated—for a time, since their time in any case was nearly up.

And what of the war-making nations? One thinks of a sinister mutuality of perfectly balanced hostilities, the leaders bickering and chattering like a cage of angry monkeys, yet, like no monkeys on earth, lying, invading, cozening, controlling, killing when expedient. They fulfilled to the letter the dark description of the inhuman set down in Paul's letter to the Christians of Rome: "They were filled with every kind of wickedness, evil, covetousness, malice"(Rom. 1:29 NRSV).

Behold their dire achievement. They continue researching, building, launching all manner of doomsday weapons. Thus the assembly of humans, in the space of a lifetime, becomes a kind of cosmic suicide club. In the process the earth is wasted, human need contemned, large numbers of people—refugees, homeless, jobless, ill—are declared expendable. Top to bottom, the ecology of creation is monstrously shaken, as is our humanity, in self-understanding, in the once solicitous heart. Morally and physically, the web is torn.

Indeed, the degradation of America serves to underscore once again the ancient stereotype and impasse of the nations described by Isaiah—imperial nests of sanctioned, perennial violence, of wars that are proclaimed "necessary" and, of course, "just." Isaiah understood his times, and ours—a world laden with memories of war and perennially prepared for another war, clumsy and indifferent in the skills of peace.

It is an unlikely time indeed to issue a word of hope and imagination. Yet, the worst time, Isaiah dares say, is the apt time! The moment to speak up is exactly that time when one is tempted to drop one's hands. This time, Isaiah declares audaciously, is exactly the apt time; time to announce the immanent toppling of the impregnable gods of war!

We are summoned to a sorry and a thankless task—fidelity to the oracle, to lay hammers against the sword. Yet we have the promise of Isaiah: the sword is turned aside, the plow renews the earth.

Whose Brows Are Darkness, Who Claim the Light
(5:8–24, 26–30)

5:8   Shame be yours
       larcenists of the land—
       parcel by parcel, tenants
       reduced to chill penury,
       despairing, evicted.

9   I swear; those great houses of yours
       will stand gaping, empty to the winds of heaven;

10   sere, fields struck with mildew and worm.

11   And shame, you
       gluttons, gormandizers, debauched ones,
       bellies full, souls parched,
       unmindful of the works of Yahweh and
       his governance.

      . . . .

13   Who will succor you
       on the day of my visitation?
       Hounding hungers
       devour you!

      . . . .

20   Shamed be you
       who revile goodness, name evil good
       whose brows are brooding darkness,
       who claim the light, whose soul dwells
       in stygian night!
               who rejoice wickedly
       when grief befits, whose sole mourning
       is loss of ill-gotten goods!

21   And shame to you
       who embrace evil

sanctimoniously sighing; Ah,
come quickly, Day of Yahweh, Rapture!

. . . .

22 Shame, you
who puff yourselves, clever fellows,
23 for a bribe set scoundrels free,
turning thumbs down on the just.
Shamed be you, one and all!
24 Even now, fires of retribution
creep toward you, consuming!
—I spell out the cause—
you dare contemn the word
of Yahweh Savior.

These curses would seem naturally to follow the song of the
vineyard in verses 1–7 (see the New Jerusalem Bible). The song
opens with a warmhearted fiction. Isaiah has a friend who has a
vineyard. Every care is expended to bring a bountiful harvest;
clearing stones, digging, planting a noble muscat grape, raising a
tower to guard the harvest, digging a pit in which to tread the
grapes. The industrious husbandman has only to await the happy
outcome of his hopes and labors. How consoling are his dreams as
day after day, the vines are blessed with favorable sun and rainfall!

Then something goes wrong, inexplicably. A canker, worms?
We have a fault in nature; no skill or industry suffices to undo it.
The facts are plain as they are painful; no harvest to speak of. Only
a mockery: sour, wizened grapes malingering on the vine.

The tone of the story changes. The "friend" who owned the
vineyard is revealed as none other than Yahweh. The implication is
plain. The vineyard is even to be punished for failing to produce.

The vineyard parable is always and everywhere applicable; to
Isaiah's time, to our own. It is a warning to keep alert in the search
for justice, the time of bloodshed notwithstanding. At times the
shedding of blood all but obliterates the faint traces of justice and
stops the searchers in their tracks. We are called to hearken to the
cries of distress, raised in courts and prisons and places of torture
and disappearance, arising from the homeless and disenfranchised
on our mean streets.

The curses of verses 8 to 24 bring the parable home, an ethical commentary on the poetry of the failed vineyard. Here, unmistakenly plain, are the ways the harvest failed.

Cursing is an ancient biblical enterprise. The "woe to" or "shame" pronounces judgment in the here and now, an anticipation, summing up, denunciation, reminder, all of these. It throws a wrench in the apparently unstoppable machinery of the worldly system.

The last and least anticipation of the powerful is that they could be thought to stand under judgment. And what a judgment it is, issued as it is by an Isaiah utterly deprived of the mechanisms of power!

First to be cursed are the land developers and builders. They pander to the rich, and so doing, become rich. They create a network of ownership and control and exclusion, raising great houses, controlling extensive farmlands and vineyards.

Behold, all for naught, their mansions remain unsold and empty, the fields and vines fall short in the yield—the vineyard event again!

One has a sense that a voracious economy is its own undoing; it soon falls flat, the real estate proves to be unreal indeed, at least in benefitting those in possession. Something akin to intensive farming has soured and thinned the soil. In sum, greed has brought scant return, even of a material sort. (Are there echoes here of megafarming with its pesticides and chemicals and abuse of the land?)

The empty houses and barren landscape are stark images of spiritual desolation. The souls of those who would be tycoons are parched. Once again, the condition of nature and of human artifacts, thriving or failing, offer apt images of the spiritual condition of ourselves.

In verses 11–13, a second "shame" is pronounced on gorging and drunkenness as a way of life. Isaiah is surely not to be construed as the forerunner of bluestockings and puritans. Something more is at stake. Frivolity breeds distraction, inattention. One becomes "unmindful of the works of Yahweh."

Missing the point and pith of life, the debauched are already in exile. Of how many among the great ones of earth, the image proves shatteringly exact! Psychology would say they are alienated from their true selves. The Bible insists differently; they become aliens and strangers before God and the community—and the world of nature as well.

Experience invites a reflection; judges and prosecutors are particularly subjects of such "shame." Woebegone indeed they are—far and away from truth, compassion, plain speech, godly sense of justice. They are under oath and offer ultimate fealty to the "law of the land." That law protects such awful scourges as racism, the scapegoating of the poor, the lawlessness of war and war preparation! Indeed, as one among their rank explained to an aggrieved woman, "Ours is a court of law, not of justice."

The law, or money, or power, or all of these have shunted the willful aside from reality—in the wrong direction, an endless detour of spirit, a dead end of illusion, fantasy, appetite. They are in exile indeed, an affliction dating perhaps from the moment when the oath of office was sworn—and "the works of Yahweh" were foresworn. The outcome is in a sense, after the fact; it illumines a situation that went before. We ponder the "shame" and its accompanying threat of exile. Do curse and threat imply that only in dire circumstances, brought low, arrogant eminences will come literally, to their senses? Parched all along, thirsting for the truth, they were deprived of the truth and ignorant of their deprivation. Only an infusion of truth could assuage it.

Who was to assuage it? Their coequals? The authorities who appointed and honored them? The church? The thirsting mind is refreshed only by a draft of the truth. Like fresh waters, truth is unpolluted by the sweet or sour of ideology. But the mind of the jurist (our example) is afflicted; it lost its native aptitude for truth, was emptied in the exercise of office, of vigor and integrity.

This is how it began. The highest authorities scrutinized likely candidates and came to a final choice. This one, they implied, is safe, can be counted on. He will pronounce the oath, and honor the law above all other consideration.

And the church? By and large, it had no refreshment to hold to the lips of the dignitary robed in black—no critique, no stern or compassionate or risky nay-saying. No word like this was offered: The oath you purpose to utter implies that the law of the land is become your idol, has seized the place of honor above the law of God, above conscience and the biblical Word. Such cannot be.

In such wise, the vocation of the church becomes manifest, as the church confronts (but also ministers to) the powers of this world.

Verse 20 shifts from images to straight moral teaching concerning the perversion of the moral sense. To do evil is one thing, roundly condemned by Isaiah and his kind. Thus to our inestimable benefit, Isaiah and his followers educate our moral sense. And more, they offer us exemplars of what they preach: the holiness of Yahweh made manifest in humans grown passionate for justice. For such blessings we give thanks.

There is a perversion worse than evil deeds. Isaiah avers it with the clarity of an open eye. It is to misname evil as goodness, to exalt it, parade it, honor it, to raise public icons of moral turpitude.

Thus in our culture (and probably in Isaiah's as well) honorifics are bestowed on warriors and tycoons and politicians and entrepreneurs. Shame is promulgated against "those who name evil good" (v. 20).

Branding goodness as evil, indicting goodness, convicting the virtuous, punishing them straitly is the tactic and ideology of the criminal justice system. Thus, the courts take their place in the war, making the state a chief principality, together with others of their kind, the military, the universities, the industrial conglomerates.

Those who claim the light while dwelling in the darkness fancy themselves that they are morally acute, superiorly enlightened, that they are granted powers beyond challenge or accountability.

Jesus often borrowed the image of blindness as he too confronted the darkness of the age. One episode is well worth the lengthy attention paid it (John 9). Jesus had healed a man who was born blind. There was no denying the miracle; yet it was expedient for his critics to proceed with fanatical denial of Jesus' authority.

The exchange is wonderfully revealing. The healed man stands firm; yes, he was blind, and yes, now he sees. Why, forsooth, do you make a great noise of this and deny the plain evidence of your eyes as well as mine?

"Or can it be" (in a quite wonderful twist of the knife) "that you want to become his disciples too?" (9:27).

His parry was enough, and too much. There was one expedient left to them, this discomfited crew. Heap scorn on the man who testified to his healing and cast him out.

Jesus seeks him out. The man, lucid and honorable to the last, confesses his faith. Jesus responds, "For judgment have I come into the world, that the blind may see and those who see become blind" (9:39).

Some who heard asked him, "What, are we blind too?"

And the shattering riposte, "If you were blind you would not be guilty of sin, but you claim you can see. So your guilt remains" (9:40–41).

It would seem, on the face of it, a fairly rudimentary moral task to call things by their name; to call light light, darkness darkness. The Bible has news for us; moral incapacity rules the world. The system does not know light from darkness.

John's Gospel applies the theme to the Great Advent: "That life was the light of humans. The light shines in the darkness, but the darkness has not understood it" (1:4–5).

Does darkness understand light? Far from it, according to Isaiah also. Darkness knows only itself. And worse, it would be in command of the light, it is voracious as the throat of hell. It must extinguish the light so that darkness only shall rule; dark minds, darkened hearts, secret pacts, covert actions, undeclared and unsanctioned wars, promises, promises, people befuddled out of their skulls, moral confusion over all.

One ought to be clear about at least a few matters—war, capital killing, aborting the unborn! Isaiah invites such clarity, and in a sense, leaves to us the conclusions, the details, the issues. But in the simple declaration (all and any behavior is not to be named good, acceptable, human, approved of God) there is great relief!

The images of human measuring of values, whether kept or violated, continue (vv. 21 and 22). The latter invites woe. Those who overstep are the prestidigitators of human fortune; they claim to turn dross into gold. The reward comes in greed fulfilled and ego refurbished. The world goes topsy-turvy; the scent of controlling power enters the brain, stimulating, fermenting there. In such a state, it seems logical and sensible that one "for a bribe, sets scoundrels free, turning thumbs down on the just."

We are offered a contrary image by Jesus (and as implied, by Isaiah as well). Drunks occupy thrones, moral inebriates bestride the world. "You know that among the nations, those in authority lord it over others" (Mark 10:42). So be it. This analysis of Jesus, placed crucially by Mark just before the passion and death, includes a stern forbidding. One senses the seriousness of the moment, the solemn tone of Jesus: "None of this among you! If one among you seeks greatness, let him serve. If one seeks to be first, let him be the slave of all" (Mark 10:43).

No sterner command was ever issued by the Master who served. No lording over, no controlling behavior, no down putting, no exalting of ego. We have touched a point of crisis, a boundary; it must not be crossed.

In so crucial a matter the disciples are hardly without an example. He stands before them, servant and slave. In a sentence or two, he commends himself to them. It is an unusual turn, for this selfless One, a moment that stops the heart, an epiphany. For them, it could be a transfiguration; at least it is so offered: "Just as the human One has come into your midst, not to be served but to serve"—and he will push the matter further, a blinding self-revelation, utterly confounding—"who has come into your midst to give his life as a ransom for all" (10:45).

We have not heard such language from him, nor indeed from any mortal. Ransom? For all? If all must be ransomed, under whom or what do we languish? And if such be our estate, how comes it we remain unconscious as to our plight?

The mind boggles. Are we offered a gift, two-edged? Are we plunged into the soundless depths of the Mystery? Who are we anyway, so bound about hand and foot, generationally enslaved?

Like Isaiah, Jesus also pronounces a series of woes (Matt. 23:13 ff.). They resemble the Isaian curses; both series are launched at the proud heads of authorities, religious or secular.

We note, too, that no such denunciations are uttered against the "little ones" of our world. The Samaritan woman of many husbands is simply appraised of Christ's knowledge of her unconventional status (John 4:17). The man languishing by the pool of Bethesda is first healed; then he is warned (John 5:14). The woman seized in adultery is snatched from death, and her prosecutors put to shame. After the episode, she is gently admonished (John 8:11).

No curses, woes, thunders. In every case, mercy and compassion are the motif.

But against the high and mighty, fire and brimstone rain from the heavens (Isa. 5:24, 25). Terrifying, the suavity and tenderness of Isaiah explode in rage. Always there is the same provocation: the justice of God, or the covenant, or the law of compassion—in sum the "word of Yahweh"—these synonymous realities have been despised and violated.

God is the witness of wickedness in high places and of sin's undoing. The invasion is imagined here as instigated by God, no other:

5:26 From afar
a fierce nation rises,
a torrid zone
blinding upon the horizon,
a lion shaking off sleep.

27 Swift, soundless, tireless,
belts buckled, sandals intact,
arrows and bows on the ready.
28 Like flints
horses' hooves strike fire,
chariot wheels
a blur, a whirlwind.
29 Deep throated
the roar of warriors, lions
seizing, dragging
prey in the dust.
"That day, My day!
Israel
be warned; tears, distress,
distemper, darkness."

The poetry hints at an analogy. The authorities, indicted as violators and cheats and purveyors of injustice, have already been "invaded." Another spirit than the spirit of God possesses and dominates them. They are fit subjects for a fiery exorcism.

2

The Vision, The Consequences

We begin here with the "call" of Isaiah the prophet. We share with him in the harsh, uncompromising assessment of our estate as the human stands face to face with the Holy One! We move from the sublime to the mundane and quotidian, from the Unknowable graciously nearing to an outcome announced beforehand, failure and ignominy. The oppositions, clashes, conundrums, things known and unknowable, as well as the furious maelstrom of divine moods—all are here.

The prophet carries out his calling, in part, by announcing the vision of Emmanuel, God with us, the one who will come fulfilling yet confounding the hopes of the people of God.

Lips Touched with Fire (6:1–13)

6:1 In the year that King Uzziah died
I beheld Yahweh
2 the seraphim surrounding—
3 in my soul their song
thrice sounding,
> **Holy One**
> **whose glory fills the earth!**
4 I could but stammer;
mercy on me, for polluted lips
and the nattering of my people!

6 An angel seized living coals
touched my mouth with fire—
7 "Now, all expunged—
announce the evangel!"
8 And the Lord God spoke;
"Whom then shall we send?
who to bear the word?"

Tongue, heart aflame I cried,
"I, I, no other!"

9 This God of ironies!
"Go then, if go you must.
This for only message;
Do you listen, people?
you hear nothing.
See, do you?
nothing upon nothing."
10 "Dullards all!
Stopped ears!
Blind eyes!
In no wise healed!"
11 And I; "How long then?"
"Until the worst;
until plague, famine—
until no hope.

12 "Until
in a scape
empty as a gorgon's yawn
one survivor stand—
13 "from a heaven-
shading oak
struck down—
living hope
sole hope
from stump of hope."

Isaiah is thus summoned. The event is staggering. His response stands above and beyond a shadow of doubt. Indeed, when doubt shortly appears, a grey shadowy eminence, it will be strictly in the mind of his hearers, not in his. It is on them that a straight, clear message of repentance and conversion will sit uneasily.

There is this to be said for (or against) this Yahweh of Isaiah: he is surely blunt of tongue! Let nothing of this blazing commerce or of its worldly outcome be left in doubt!

The transcendent One implicitly and from the start knows the outcome. To God's word will be granted neither success nor fair hearing nor responsive obedience.

In a flash the chosen one is appointed and placed, not in some ideal believing community, but amid the principalities of the world. Isaiah, like Jeremiah and Ezekiel and Daniel, must make his way through a gauntlet of hostility and rancor. This is where you, Isaiah, belong, which is to say, in the rank of the failures, the scorned and ignored, even the martyrs.

It is harsh news indeed. But in a sense, it is no news at all. The truth he is sent to announce will perennially be placed in question, in contention, in balance, in jeopardy.

This might even be thought a workable definition of the "systems" of the world—a locus, a people among whom the truth is more or less negotiable, essentially weightless, without moral consequence, arguable, subject to jotting and tittling, even disposable. We have other resources; who needs this "word of God"?

On a scene rife with sin and dark opinion, with authority uncommended and violence in command, arrives one who knows. What is known is a truth that is not been the fruit of rational argument or natural theology. The truth as granted is a vision imposed, beyond denial or doubt, sovereign. It is a gift, pure gift, the blazing image and icon of what we name religious faith. It is the sight of Yahweh and the burning coal.

We are granted no inkling of Isaiah's life prior to his vision. It is as though to his own eyes nothing worth recording happened prior to the summons. Here and in the subsequent oracles is no hint that a conversion of note preceded the vision.

He cries out a confession of sin. But this would seem to imply nothing more than sages and saints have known through the ages—the holiness of God casts into shadow everything human, including our presumed virtue.

Isaiah is sent in principle to his own, to bring unwelcome news: their claim, whether it be to a "chosen" estate, or a faithful following of covenant, is null and void. Their moral conduct is reprehensible, their worship an empty show.

He is to bring this message, as a kind of father confessor holding them to a public repentance. He is to enlarge on it; the specifics of their sin: injustice, militarism, greed, aping the nations, making the covenant a dead letter. Abandoning covenant, they have lost the God of covenant.

A sorry spectacle ensues. The gods have laid claim to the moral emptiness, like a cave invaded by errant winds have, filled the social soul with incoherence and darkness.

The prophet is also sent to the nations. Thus the horizon of religious understanding widens majestically. He is to speak of the generosity of Yahweh, God's passionate love for all. The Isaian vista is worldwide, even cosmic in scope, enchantingly so, "Unto the farthest isles" (see Isa. 24:15; 51:5).

The narrowed glance widens; the possessive exclusive scope of the older vision is ruptured. For the first time it will be asserted with full confidence that the works of creation and redemption are one. In the summons of Isaiah a splendid seed of understanding is sown. All are summoned, all peoples, all generations, all creation; love beckons.

The angels are present in full splendor. They are beings apart (as the rabbis insist). These celestial beings are wonderfully earthy. They are modest—wings cover their sex (feet); reverential—wings cover their eyes lest they see God (we are told elsewhere) and are destroyed. They have yet other wings for flying, a hint of litheness and freedom from bodily impediment. Do the angels offer clues as to our own eventual estate, the resurrection of the body? We are given only hints, enticing, thought-provoking. In the vision, they are neither intermediaries nor messengers. More in the nature of emanations, they are spirits underscoring and heightening, a foil of the Glory, insistent in their one song, "Holy One, whose glory fills the earth!"

"Holy" implies something entirely serious—another side of

things. One cannot join the majestic chorus of truth except by a wrenching turning away from the "other" song line, the glory given to idols. To chariots and to silver, as Isaiah says (see 2:7), "The land is full of these," and, finally, completing the unholy trinity, and declaring the spiritual meaning of lubricious greed and violence, "The land is full of idols" (see 2:8).

By joining the chorus of the "holy," one declares that other chant—struck up, deafening, cacophonous, by "the nations" and their sedulous apes—for what it is, "unholy, unholy, unholy."

Yet such a song is possible, and even probable, and, worst of all, actual, as Isaiah knows it, and the knowledge is both torment and spur. Humans rend the glory of God to sticks and stones.

We are in the midst of such awful obfuscations today. Indeed, the imperium is constantly multiplying both occasions and symbols of idolatry, whether in the summons to war or the enticements of appetite. More is better—more comforts, more money, more killing!

Thus the religious sense is in need of constant renewal of heart, a turning aside from the works of our hands, which proffer such spurious validity, a kind of dark imprimatur conferred on them by the hucksterings and vagaries of the culture.

Is it the law of the Fall that where there is shown an epiphany of the holy, a world of dazzle, rapturous and pristine, there will also coincide, all but collide, great darkness?.

The people (ourselves) will be favored by no such vision, in all likelihood. When we hear it reported, we will take the mystic's word for it, this holiness pressing upon him like the hand of a second creator.

Then comes the consequence of the vision, an infusion of the Spirit blowing about the world like a searing sirocco, the Spirit of justice. We will take Isaiah's word for this—or we will not. The darkness clouds the response to the vision. Yes or no, obedience or the stiff neck?

Isaiah diagnoses our illness with probes of steel. Luther could hardly be more explicit, more dour, "reformist," prolapsarian, as to our condition. We are blind, deaf, sere of heart. There lies on our nature a curse. The worldly system will grind on, unhalted, unchallenged for the greater part, approved by the vast majority of humans. The system will enlist, ingest into their guts of iron, ourselves.

What then happens with the word of God that even through us would judge all systems, find them wanting and empower the great refusal? Such a word will pass us by, a whisper on a vagrant breeze. It will pass us by, if we choose.

Is there an easement of this harsh, seemingly universal, seemingly hopeless version of our soullessness, banality, guile, our tedious recalcitrance? Has there been, might there be, an exception in our midst, rising above our native incapacity for truth, our malice?

That there is, is implied here—it is the prophet himself. How ironic—it is Isaiah and his like who both announce the curse and turn back the curse. Thus he affirms—and denies.

He stands by his statement; no one will listen and obey. At the same time his very existence, his access to truth, the God he speaks for—these stand against the statement.

All is lost; all is not lost.

We note the logic beyond logic, and we rejoice. Because he has said that all is lost, and because his statement is truthful, it follows that some among us are saved, are holy, and there remains a possibility and a hope of redeeming us.

The deepest source of hope is the God of Isaiah. Otherwise, why summon the prophet at all? Why not let things fall of their awful downward pull, their own weight and dark inclination?

Thus we have the situation. God, showing and telling. God's diagnosis of human illness is conveyed, to one, to a few. Tell them (they won't listen in any serious way; tell them anyway). Tell them they are doomed, that their illness is terminal. There will always be the slaughter of wars and the crushing of the innocent.

That "always" will enter the souls of the living and persuade them beyond doubt that human fate is signed, sealed, and delivered over—to death.

Yet—and yet. The illness is terminal, and it is not terminal. The impervious door opens, a crack; light enters the dwelling of the dead. Arise!

In each generation is born a saving handful, hearing, speaking up. No generation, for all compounded wickedness, is left to its private and public kindling of hell. Thus the word is true, the awful news holds true.

Yet despite all, it is "good news" for two reasons. One, it is truthful beyond our own capacity, which leans entirely toward self-deception. Two, because the word, although concerning a universal plight, admits of an altogether crucial exception—hope.

We watch the exception take form between the lines, unacknowledged but there to be seen, implied in the words, "Go then. . . . Do you listen, people? You hear nothing. See, do you? Nothing upon nothing" (v. 9).

The Isaiah who speaks the words has first hearkened to them with all his heart. Had the message not first penetrated him, to make of him a truthful witness, of what worth were his words? He has kept on looking and has come to understanding. If not, we would hold him in low regard, a curiosity, a parrot on a perch.

The senses of the people, hearts, ears, eyes, are quite literally fallen from their proper function (v. 10). They (we) are reduced to the state of moral zombies, sleepwalking the world. This is the truth of our condition, verified on every hand. Blind, deaf, and, worst of all, heartless. Our depredations, the stench of blood, are evident across the world.

Once more, there is the exception, the one who is not fallen—not deaf, dumb, blind. Or, better, he is fallen like all of us and is resurrected from moral death. Isaiah, his heart sensitive, his ears acute, his eyes set on truth, lives and speaks. The truth he utters, but for his speaking, is as far from our ken as the farthest star from our sight.

Isaiah becomes something other than an unattainable icon. He becomes the measure of our own possibility of seeing, hearing, understanding with the heart, of being healed. Against all odds, against the crushing odds death holds, the "holy" lives in Isaiah and in those who, like him, take the word of God seriously.

The coal is lifted from the fire and held to his lips. Thus the fire of godliness is passed on and on. A community, a circle about the fire, is not merely warmed by the fire, but touched by the fire, marked indelibly.

Some would see things differently, going through the motions of this or that desultory liturgy. Hearts are elsewhere, words void, gestures all of appeasement, of bad faith. Perhaps this God of ours can be cajoled, persuaded to stand with us, with our armies, our gross national product, our pentagon, our world markets, our

NAFTA stretching ever farther, continental and worldwide, insatiable, predatory. Perhaps this God is amenable to fine words, songs, gestures, coins raining down, grandiloquent art and architecture. Perhaps Yahweh is like us, a godfather tut-tutting our little weaknesses. Perhaps our God can be hoodwinked.

Inevitably, the vision fades. The prophet may have been wrapt apart for a moment or for many hours. Time is no measure, holds no meaning here. Then it seems as though he utters a great sigh. Now he must face the ironbound systems of this world. The work of faith must be taken up, hefted to shoulder, like a hundredweight.

The vision has its price. This is proof of its being genuine. Speak the truth, Isaiah, in fair weather and foul. For all his life, he will pay up, and dearly.

The lips of Jeremiah are also touched, by Yahweh himself, "to place there God's words" (1:9). He has nonetheless, a terrible time acceding to his vocation. There is a more realistic scene in Ezekiel; he is commanded to "eat the scroll of Yahweh's word" (3:3).

To biblical faith there remain only small gestures of mitigation, of resistance, of unmasking, of holding accountable. In a stunning modern midrash, Isaiah's beating of swords into plowshares is translated time and again—in the pouring of blood, the blows of small hammers, the largely symbolic damage or interference to "murder as usual."

Isaiah agreed to the charge of Yahweh, fruitless as it appeared and without issue. He obeyed, with the promptitude of the naive or the seasoned and holy, or perhaps of both. He responded to the question, "Whom then shall we send?" with the bold affirmation, "I, I, no other."

This is no lark, no lighthearted venture of a summer's day. Let me tell you what lies ahead. This is a work that goes—nowhere. For all your pains, it will bring not reward or gratitude but scorn, contumely. Indeed it will be argued by many, and heatedly, that you will succeed only in worsening the condition of an already inflamed and splenetic people. Hearts, due to your dire bent, will further harden. They will bristle at your approach. You dabble in matters beyond you, endanger the common weal. Despite the best intention, you will bestow a spurious credential on the ugliest elements of the populace.

Worse and worse, an anathema is inevitable. You presume for yourself the word of God, immemorially entrusted to priesthood and temple. Dare you thus blaspheme?

Your last hours will be feverish with voices. Was your chosen course foolish or wise?

Foolish, destructive, what awful forces you set loose!

Emmanuel: To Choose and Be Chosen (7:13–17)

The strange and wonderful sign given in Isaiah 7 has become the subject of a vast millennial Christian midrash, in scripture and liturgy and popular devotion. The sign surpasses utterly the current denizen of the throne of Judah; it is as though he has no personal existence or credential beyond that of the royal line. How those kings have vexed, sinned against God and humans! Thus the "house of David" is majestically addressed:

7:13   Hearken then
       you of David's line—
       How you weary, yes,
       the patience of God!

14   "Nonetheless. A sign.
       A young maid, pregnant,
       bears a son, Emmanuel.

15   "On milk and honey he feeds,
       right reason flowers, and he
       unerring chooses goodness only.

       . . . .

17   "Meantime, awful time!
       such horrors, abominations
       as never fell to humans!

       And you will know why."

In the episode culminating in this wondrous vision of Emmanuel, Isaiah faces a crisis, brought about by the machinations of his ruler. In verses 1–9, the scene is reconstructed. A foreign coalition is mounted against Jerusalem. Details need not detain us; the story is as old as the forging of the first sword, and ultimately as banal. What did the first sword, what did all subsequent swords, what will the hypothetical last sword of all serve to accomplish? Such questions are raised by the oracle, even to us, over whom the nuclear sword has hovered uneasily for a lifetime.

King Ahaz is terrified, and the people with him, "palpitating, as the trees of the forest palpitate under a wind" (7:2). The king goes berserk. We are told elsewhere (2 Kings 16:1–9) of the awful details. He sacrifices his son to the gods and prepares for armed conflict. For such acts he stands condemned by the author of Kings. A moral gloss lies upon him and his ilk, one after another.

The crisis worsens. Isaiah is summoned by God to confront the besotted king. "Go to him, and take along your son, named 'Some Will Return' [or 'The Remnant']" (7:3)—a touch both tender and exact. A name dear to Isaiah's hope is already conferred on the son of his heart.

What a contrast! One son is sacrificed to the gods of war, another, signifying hope and endurance, accompanies his father on a mission of truth.

Isaiah stands before God, under obedience to deliver a hard message. We are edified by his prompt response. Summoned, he goes on the moment. Clearly he risks status and access for the sake of fidelity to the truth entrusted to him.

The instruction to the demoralized king could hardly be more exact, detailed, curt. First, Isaiah offers an analysis of the situation, which is sufficiently serious. A conspiracy has been mounted: a tyrant plans to invade, displace Ahaz, and install a more complaisant client on the throne.

In the face of this threat, Isaiah's message is not to fear: "This shall not be" (7:7). There is divine contempt for the machinations and drum beats of the giants at the gate. We shall bring these great ones down to proper size. They are, after all, no more than human; no, they are less, they are hollow men, all mock-up and show. The image of the invaders is ironic, down putting; the foreigners are "no more dangerous than the smoke from two smoldering sticks of wood" (7:4).

Just as the scorn toward the military powers is voiced, so also is a warning to Ahaz, an "if," even a veiled threat: "If your faith in me is not enduring, you will not endure at all" (7:9). Indeed, Yahweh knows the heart, our circumventions, cowardice—our need.

We are at the heart of biblical faith. The faith that animates Isaiah and sends him on his errand is the faith he commends to the watery-kneed Ahaz. Such faith is less a matter of believing God exists than a practiced trust, under whatever pressure. We are in a world (Isaiah's, our own) rife with evidence contrary to stirrings of trust. On the occasion that faces Isaiah and the king (on any such occasion before and since), the authorities have every reason, drawn from available evidence as well as the counsel of experts, to shift their trust away from God. Trust in God is for children and women and the naive—for pacifists. It will suffice for normal times, for occasional religious gestures.

But when the chips are down, we must trust in the sword. Say it loud and clear; there is no other recourse. Surely our cause is just, the enemy is the aggressor. And so on.

What of Isaiah? Why not assure the king that indeed his conclusion is sensible, that the war impending is a just war? Among other benefits, would not such advice mortise one's own position as a seer whose good sense is intact? Raise a hand in blessing. Let the war drums rattle.

Quite possibly among those so-called experts at the king's ear would be found a coterie of court prophets whose counsel would go exactly along such lines.

Not Isaiah. The word is abrupt, unmodified, take or leave. Hold firmly to Yahweh; no other lifeline will hold.

It is, after all, a matter of trust as well as a matter of the betrayal of trust. One has not really (that is, in the biblical sense) said in one's heart, "God exists" until one has said, "I trust you." The first assertion is notional, abstract, a matter perhaps of natural theology, the mind laboring at its logic. The second is a communion, bread on the tongue from an unseen hand. The first can be uttered in all good faith, even as one takes the contrary evidence as decisive (sword against sword, just causes from Ahaz to Clinton). The second is a heavy burden of denial of all that: "You have spoken, I cannot know the outcome. I obey nonetheless."

Trust me, trust not arms. Are we to conclude from this word

springing from the Isaiah-Ahaz crisis that the God of Isaiah is non-violent? Can we affirm this despite the carnage elsewhere reported in Scripture as divinely sanctioned?

If such is not the newness and purity of the Isaian vision of the God who says simply to the king; swords into plowshares, here and now—if not this, what conclusion befits?

The story of the first encounter ends here; we learn from other sources that Isaiah's message to the king was ill received. Ahaz embraced military disaster as well as the gods of the nations.

Yahweh tries again, offering a second sign, this one more sublime and direct, offered without the intervention of the prophet. Ahaz is even invited to seek a sign, even a sign that might be drawn from hell or high heaven, something beyond imagining, supersensible, something impossible to human ingenuity or skill. Was it at this period that poor Ahaz had embraced idols? If so, the proffer of Yahweh has a particular poignancy; Yahweh is searching a way to bring to his senses a deviant, bellicose, weak, idolatrous ruler.

Something then beyond the scope of your pantheon, your war gods! A gift. Ask it; it shall be yours. A sign will be given—a child called Emmanuel. In the face of all, God is with us.

The Tender Stream and the Turbulent Hearts
(8:6–8,11–18)

8:6   The waters of Shiloah
      softly go,
   gentle as dawn upon their flowing,
   tender as lisping children.

7   But in your hearts no echo
   of murmurous currents—
   no will to peacefulness!

8   Your hearts a torrent, a torment!

   Do I name you Emmanuel
   (misnaming you utterly!)
   you, your multiple gods
   your strife and warring?

See, my hand
stirs the wild rivers from sleep,
warriors dreaming of war!
Uncontained they sweep you away,
bestride you like Pharaoh's hordes,
utterly whelm you under!

The genius is in the irony of the oracle; it is as Emmanuel that the recusant people are addressed. And God ponders, can the name "God With Us" be rightly conferred on those who choose to be without God? What a misnomer, God reflects in considerable bitterness of soul.

Yet the nations threatening God's people will fare no better than the faithful (8:9–10). It is as though God were saying, a pox on both your houses. You resemble one another intolerably—the godless nations and the godless "Emmanuel." You both believe, not in me but in war. Your trust is not in me but in arms.

There will be war indeed, in accord with the termagancy of both sides. But there will be no winners. Let the faithless, the formerly faithful, know this: the God who "is with us" allows no misuse of the name Emmanuel as a war cry.

Then Isaiah turns to his own. This is the first indication that he is supported by a little band of disciples. The occasion is a stern one; the crisis demands the strengthening of his community, of those whose strength is elsewhere than in the aggressions of the powerful. This passage is uniquely apt to the aspirations of the nonviolent:

8:11   As a net falls
upon a sparrow
so Yahweh seized my soul
turn, turning me away
away from the ways of this people;

12   Spurn utterly the schemes
of the great intriguers;
Have no fear!

13   I am Yahweh.
      Me you shall fear, no other.

14   I am a stone; the people stumble.
      No, a boulder; I break them asunder.
15   A trap, a net; they bumble and tumble—
      head over heels. Caught.

16   Isaiah, press the word close,
      a tattoo on your soul;
17   God has fled the faithless.

      But for your part, wait on Yahweh,
      in him your trust.

18   Here beside my children,
      gifts of Yahweh—
          behold us
      signs and portents before Israel.

Here is surely one of the tenderest passages in all prophecy! The little ones (as well as the great parent) are portents, signs, presages, prophetic presences. They are simply "children, gifts of Yahweh." Together with their father, they are evidence before a faithless people of Yahweh's love, compassion, providence. The generations will not fail; the precious human substance is not to be lost.

Not even war can wreak such final havoc. This is by way of promise, the rainbow arches above the deluge.

The presence of children makes the faithlessness we name war particularly heinous. The children are our future. When the guns take aim at them, we make war on the future; we despise and destroy the least protected, the most vulnerable of the human fauna. The children are a clue. Will the clue be read aright?

The days are filled with anxiety. Chips are down, the king has decided on war. But the true believers are to have no fear; do not fear what the faithless fear. To yield here, to be possessed by fear, is to kill.

No matter the boom of big guns nearing, no matter the faithless ones who aim and discharge them. The little band of disciples is to stand firm, take heart, as the father does, as children do, in mutual and spontaneous trust.

We are Emmanuel. Remember? God is with us.

God is with us not as the god of war. God is with us in the refusal of war. And the children are the sign of this holy presence. Can we imagine little children plotting, making war?

In these mad times we can imagine child warfare, adolescent warfare—because we see it in such bizarre and blood-ridden days as we endure. In the cities the children make war on one another. Early and earlier in life they become the observant, even sedulous apes of ourselves. They bear our guns in their hands, our wickedness in their hearts. What a poisoned legacy!

They are no longer an image of the children of Isaiah; they cannot be brought forward as argument against war and killing. They are fast becoming a sign not of the God of peace but of the gods of war.

And yet, and yet, a later Emmanuel will one day declare: "Unless you become as one of these, the least of mine, you will not enter the realm of God" (Matt. 18:3).

We sometimes speak of growing out of childhood. It is usually to our loss. We grow out of childhood—into war. We grow out of the God of childhood into homage toward the gods of war. The gods of our adulthood are diplomatic, which is to say glib, mendacious, insipid, tedious, mealymouthed. Or they are bellicose—truculent, cocksure, grisly, treacherous, callous, ferocious. One kind or another, such gods drive us toward moral oblivion.

The poet Yehuda Amichai has God showing mercy to children, and no mercy toward adults. Is this because adults show so little mercy?

> God has pity on kindergarten children.
> He has less pity on school children.
> And on grownups he has no pity at all,
> he leaves them alone,
>
> and sometimes they must crawl on all fours
> in the burning sand
> to reach the first-aid station
> covered with blood . . .

The Child Named Hope (9:1, 2–7; 11:1–9)

9:1   Darkness is not all,
        Nor war the last word;
        not by a long shot, or a short.

        The children speak it;
        the last word. Hope.
        Hope; the children.

        The Child.

The Child! He sums up in his entitlement the best of our sorry race; the wisdom of Solomon, the tenderness of Anna and the life-giving mothers, the courage of David, the genius of Moses and the liberators, and, yes, Isaiah himself and the mystics.

9:2   The people who walked in darkness
        have seen a great light
        at long last dawn.

   3   You   You   You
      joy   harvest   wealth

   4   the yoke weighed heavy
      the oppressors prodding
        hither   yon
        us   beasts   of   burden

   5   boots
      trod us under
      blood reeking armor
      Look!
      all for naught
      rot   rust
6a   child wrought this
      a son

His the power the glory
hagios athanatos
holy deathless One
iskyros strong One
emmanuel God with us

wisdom from on high
prince of peace
desired
of the everlasting hills

7   we pray
make firm
plant deep
justice, peace
now and forever

amen alleluia

Christians, in a daring midrash, will claim these great titles for our Christ. Would that the seizure had been in accord with the spirit of the titles, especially "Prince of Peace"!

What is to be said about tears and blood spent since that time of genetic disaccord, when it became clear that "our Christ" was not to be "their Christ"?

11:1 From a barren stump
this tender shoot—
The One who is, is to come!
2   My servant, in him
spirit of counsel, of strong resolve,
of sure knowledge, of the fear of Yahweh.
3   For the little ones, the remnant
justice his passion.
4   His tongue lashes the violent
his breath a flame
consuming the wicked—
5   righteousness, fidelity

a cincture binding him close.

6 That day, My day
   the wolf, the lamb
   side by side,
   the leopard, the goat—
   calf and lion feeding together
   and a little child
   hither and yon
   leading them
7 The cow, the bear—
   their young side by side,
   lions meek as lambs
     feeding, imagine!
     on the ox's straw
8 an infant
   deep, fast asleep
   in a viper's nest

9 No ravening wars, no evil
   the land like a placid sea

   tidal, susurrating,
   permeated, animated
   with knowledge of Yahweh!

   Is Isaiah's vision beyond words? It is at once unitive, oneiric, pristine, and tender. In light of it, how can any say the Bible is ecologically unconcerned, or worse?

3

The Tyrant's Motto: "Seize the Day; It Is Worth Two Tomorrows"

Throughout the oracles of Isaiah against the various foreign peoples, the "nations," whose lands surrounded Judah and who threatened her at one time or another, are warnings and promises to Judah. Details about what will come are lacking. Thus, we are well advised to concentrate on essentials: Yahweh's work with Israel is a work of liberation—personal, spiritual, social.

The nations, the great imperial superstates, of course are involved in the mysterious process as Israel becomes grist for the mills of the godlings. For a millennium the purifying, the slow emergence of a certain version of self-conscious humanity goes on. What is a human being, a human community?

There are opposing versions of the human, devastatingly alike—Babylon, Egypt, Assyria, Rome. One after another they rise and shine with splendor. One after the other they flourish, devastate, invade, plunder, enslave; and, learning nothing, they fall.

Meantime, their common version of the human is taken up again and again, blindly employing greed, violence, injustice. One after another, they raise and unsheathe the instruments of awful actualities, the flails and swords of human history. On rampage, like blind and besotted giants they wreak suffering, enslavement, exile, ecological devastation, death abrupt and slow.

What of Israel? A third-rate power, this people can easily be destroyed. Yet amid all turmoil and disaster, the prophets insist that God is at work, against all odds and appearances to the contrary.

The incalculable resource the prophets offer, simply, and to speak personally, is to keep us going. Their offering speaks to all we come to value and honor. They address the questions of our own soul: What is a human being today? What is human behavior? They counsel us in our life with others to strive to create, even in modest measure, community, the convergence and concentrate of the tradition.

The Kings in Hell (14:4–21)

14:4   To this has he come, the tyrant?
       to dead end, his arrogance?
  5   Yahweh broke him, a dry stick—
       broken scepter, broken bones.
  6   In hell
       The great braggart and blight
          wavers, staggers forward,
         a face of cobweb—
         a skinny shade,
         ragtag, tattered.

  . . . .

  9   The shadowy kings of earth
       all astir, dead leaves in a breeze above.
       A reveille of ghosts!
         Up from their rickety thrones
       (the bones conjoint of victims'
       hip bones, thigh bones)
         phantasmagoric, doomed
         the kings arise,
  10   this their jibing chorus,
         "You too,
       like us in crime and consequence,
       like us annihilated!
  11   Welcome, regent,
       to bed of maggots, coverlet of worms."

12 "Fallen, fallen, star of morning,
     darling of dawn, world conqueror—
     wormwood, gall your portion!

13 You said in your heart,
     'Mine the heights
     where clouds and winds conceive.
     Mount Olympus my seigniorage—
14   I,   I,   I,
     like unto the Most High!'"

15 Eccolo, prone you lie—
     paradigm and pith of hell.
16 The shades gape and peer;
     "Is this the shaker and breaker
     merciless, captor, raptor,
17 who made of sweet earth a desert
     and called it peace?

18 "No tomb for you, ordure, offal,
     a foul ditch your dwelling.
 . . . .
20 "Be nameless forever,
     wrecker, ravener,
          weighed, found wanting.
21 Null. A nothing."

This magnificent *mashal* was, we are told, in all probability composed by Isaiah himself against Nebuchadnezzar. It is an unsurpassed example of Isaiah down-putting illegitimate power.

Sojourns in the world of the dead are fairly frequent in ancient mythology. Isaiah is probably drawing on Phoenician texts, the themes of which later are reflected in Greek and Latin classics. The sixth book of the *Aeneid* comes to mind, but with a difference. In the sojourn of Virgil's hero, the shadowy dead receive him respectfully. Here, the reception of the wicked ruler is furious, humiliating, laced with scorn and contumely.

For this one there is no celestial journey in a boat of gold to the heart of the sun, to immortality. Isaian scorn follows him, deposed and exposed, to the underworld.

The God of the living, Yahweh, is envisioned first as the tender restorer of his own. Not only that, but in a strict tit for tat, those who once enslaved Israel will themselves be enslaved.

Isaiah never quite loses a sense of God the just, as well as God the compassionate One—even when anger (divine or Isaian, not easily distinguished)—all but extinguishes the sun in the sky!

The Counselors Confounded (19:1–15)

19:1 See, idols topple—
   the fiery gaze of Yahweh!

   . . . .

 5 earth groaning
   great rivers fouled

   . . . .

 7 pleasant savannahs forests primeval
   reeking
  harvests choked with thorn
 8 empty nets boats rotting
   lamentation
 9 the poor unsuccored
   landless profitless
   friendship soured
 10 searing enmity
   blade against blade
   unaccountable
   death the marauder
  scythe at ready

   . . . .

 11 governance adrift tyranny overbearing
  where the wisdom where relief

   . . . .

 13 fools enthroned
  warriors witless

14   counselors confounded
         drunk they are
         foundering   reeling   vomiting
         vertiginous   vain
15   caducous
         see
                scepter and crown
                tumbling down

The prophet offers a close analysis of a certain kind of society. Its citizens are commonly regarded and regard themselves as fortunate indeed. They are prosperous, blessed by nature, politically free, and by and large engaged in works commonly considered to be virtuous.

Their situation alas, will hardly withstand serious scrutiny. The people are idolaters, and so are their leaders. They have been paying tribute to death, and to that degree they are spiritually dead.

In an idolatrous culture, someone of the spiritual stature of an Isaiah must needs stand alone. No matter if he must shout into the winds, shout he will. The truth is that an entire social fabric is woven around the practice of idolatry. It is as though splendid robes were designed and spun and woven and draped around the venerated images. The robes, let us say, change with liturgical regularity. The images of priesthood are clothed splendidly, as the temple establishment makes a show of power, demonstrates its unrivaled access to the holy. Or the judiciary is honored in robe, pomp, and ceremony, or the bedizened military and its manly exploits. Or the tycoons, their ancestral portraits gracing the almighty coin of the realm. Or it is the "discoverers" of the continent or the "founding fathers" of the political system who are celebrated in myth, deemed viable and final in perfection.

When the truth approaches, the idols "tremble" on their pedestals (19:1 NRSV). The truth is unbearable to the massive illusion they embody. Their trembling often takes the form of absolute fury, the anger that conceals (and reveals) an unbearable truth; to wit, the reign of the idols is ended.

Often the fury takes official, juridical form, as in the sentences meted out time and again to those who "speak the truth to power," as in the Plowshares antimilitary actions—actions inspired, be it noted, by Isaiah and his prophecy concerning the beating of swords into plowshares.

Likewise, the hearts of the artificers, possessors (and possessed), the hucksters and worshippers of the idols fail within them. They have entrusted everything to the idols, invested everything in them—income, professional repute, and skills. Need one add that in a mad race toward power they have also invested the lives of children.

All elements of the culture are shaken; idols of repression and greed are unmasked, crimes against humanity and ecology revealed. Some years ago, we saw just such a morbidly perverse situation in American policies. Faced with the peace overtures of Gorbachev, the panic and cynicism could not have been greater if he had declared his intent to initiate a nuclear war instead of a comprehensive peace. In fact, a decision on his part to declare nuclear war might have evoked a horrid glee in our midst.

One had a sense in such days of a fragile hope. A dark, even demonic caricature of hope had been toppled; I mean the hope that the Russians would prove as evil as we had concluded they were, as evil as the weapons of each side, mirror to mirror image, declare the opponent to be.

Domestic conflict follows on idolatry. This is a capital point with Isaiah; the idols cannot set human arrangements aright. Like ourselves, the idols are warriors, racists, sexists. The images urge us to extremes—to lethal competition, to greed, to a malevolent eminence in the world.

In the book of Revelation a kind of conglomerate frenzy seizes on the superpowers one after another. Babylon would best Assyria, and Egypt would absorb both. Finally, Rome arises, a composite, a political and economic conglomerate, nightmarish, improbable in nature, horrifyingly actual—the "Beast."

For the evangelist John and his suffering community, Rome incorporates the symbols, even as it surpasses the military skills and economic greed of its predecessors. It has absorbed all—and it has learned nothing.

Behold the social consequences of idolatry. Little remains of what we come to know as traditional virtue. One against the other, whether at large or one to one, becomes the norm; not one for the other, one with the other, one succoring the other, certainly not one giving his life for another.

It cannot be stated too strongly: idolatry does not stop short in the sanctuary, nor is it confined to an hour of Sunday nor to the week-long wheeling and dealing in centers of commerce. Something more is at stake—the decline and fall of a culture. The biblical data are far-reaching, devastating. The toppling of the idols symbolizes and announces the imminent end of empire.

The Isaian logic goes something like this: When the true God is honored, the idols fall; when idols are honored, the culture falls. Isaiah is correct in more directions than one, insisting as he does on the heart of the matter, that idolatries raise a spiritual as well as a cultural question. Speaking of ourselves, the nuclear weapons' frenzy is not one of technique gone mad nor cold war divagation nor an evil empire confronting a virtuous one. It is a question of idolatry.

The primary relationship of existence, the covenant between the God of life and ourselves (and thereby between ourselves and creation) is ruptured. The consequences, as we come to know, are not slow to arrive. Nothing, literally nothing of life, nothing of community or work or humane economics or ecology, can flourish.

Thus, while public structures rot and miscarry and malfunction and misery multiplies, the authorities remain politically untouched by public anger, astonishingly popular cultural icons. The skills of those who are the mouthpieces of the idols, the sorcerers, mediums, and wizards (19:3) make the idolatrous arrangements plausible. Indeed through the machinations of these short-term and short-cut magicians, the decisions of authorities, however awful, cruel, vindictive, greedy, are made to appear wise, persuasive, even popular.

One thinks of the necromancers known as the media. Fed with enormous monies, they huckster images of appetite aroused and assuaged, of justifiable wars, of virtue at the helm of state. Voters are swung about like vanes in high wind, the bewildered multitudes are swayed this way and that. And the polls mount a mighty shout of "Yea!"

Historically, Egypt fell to the Assyrians and for a generation groaned under the heel of foreign tyrants. Could not our own predicament also be understood under this image, subject to a "foreign tyranny," "strange gods," wreaking havoc on whatever summons traditional decency, compassion, and generosity? Other gods have claimed the culture. Sometime shortly after the Civil War, the strange gods of empire entered the land with a rush. It was the beginning of an apocalypse of power and dominion—and ruin. We have never succeeded in casting off that foreign spirit that holds us in tight bondage.

We have also known the presence and felt on our bones the whiplash (and this not in times long past) of "a hard master and a fierce king" (19:4 NRSV). Indeed, a succession of such masters has waged war in the world, wreaking social injustice at home, always under the cover of the ideology of beneficence and altruism.

With regard to such matters, consult the street people, the homeless, the prisoners, those on death row, then the families barely making it, then the middle class on its own slippery slope—consult these as to the harshness of the master.

A few fortunate, and awful of mind and heart, flourish under the hard master; the wealthy grow wealthier, the conglomerates batten, the military is cozened and fed fat in vast incursions into national resources.

In verses 5 through 8 the oracle recalls an ancient biblical insight—the linkage between social morality and the good or sorry estate of the natural world. In this case, the Nile is seen as the prime source of prosperity, indispensable to the flourishing of textile industries. Alas, as the prophet notes, the river is failing. Workers, farmers, weavers, fisherfolk—all are in mourning; misery and unemployment mount.

We see the Isaian insight verified cruelly today. Nature cannot flourish while exploitation and neglect abound beyond accountability. Nature's revenge takes the form of the failure of resources, nature's God thus abandoning, cursing, departing from us, leaving to us a ruined empery.

The workers are pictured as saddened, disheartened, and powerless. Yet they do not rise up. They grow resigned; an atmosphere of blank fatalism prevails. Do they ever think to follow the trail of ruin—straight (or crooked) that leads to the palace door, the palace which is also a temple?

An extraordinarily vitriolic analysis follows in verses 11 through 15. It focuses on the authorities. Through their decisions, social crimes are inevitable; they assault the natural world and insult the God of creation. Isaiah is relentless; expressions of scorn and despising multiply:

fools enthroned
   warriors witless
     counselors confounded
       drunk they are
 foundering   reeling   vomiting
 vertiginous   vain

(19:13–14)

Finally, in verse 15, we see "scepter and crown tumbling down." Top to bottom, palace to hut, nothing works to human advantage, nothing flourishes.

Despite all this, in verses 16–25 hope is the great overriding theme. A kind of peaceable conquest of Egypt by Judea is envisioned. We have an Exodus imagery applied anew. God is now presented, ironically, as the liberator of Egypt. Egypt is also "My people." In that day, the ancient enemies, Egypt and Israel, will be reconciled by God's blessing.

When one recalls the detestation Isaiah and his like held toward Egypt, the compassion and universality of the oracle are all the more remarkable. It is a great theme for our tormented era as well.

The oppressor nations (as we know well and bitterly) are also in dire need of "a savior and champion, who will deliver them" (19:20). The oppressors are oppressed in turn. Wars and the enslavement of others diminish the common humanity, crush their people with taxation, military encroachment, domestic violence. The tables are thus turned on those who once accounted themselves insuperable.

The gentile nation is to be stricken by reason of its social crimes, then healed. It is as though Isaiah (or his later counterpart) were deliberately miming the history of Israel. Providence, finally, knows no favorites, but exerts itself on behalf of all.

We have seen like wondrous events in recent years. We have seen the massive efficacy of nonviolence in bearing the historical hopes of people to fruition, throughout Eastern Europe and the former Soviet Union and South Africa. In the unlikeliest places a degree of hope arises, in the Philippines and North Ireland and Palestine.

Finally, the blessing once conferred solely on Israel embraces all: "Blessed be my people Egypt, Assyria the work of my hands, and Israel my heritage" (19:25).

The implication seems clear. We are encouraged, emboldened, to translate: "Blessed be my people of Russia, of China, the work of my hands, of the United States my heritage."

In an astonishing act of God, the least likely event will come to pass. Swords will be beaten into plowshares. This is the great promise; the superpowers, those intransigent principalities, will undergo a change of heart. They will grow human, peaceable, just. One and all, they will renounce destructive idolatries of power and violence.

We discern here and there unprecedented, unpredictable break-throughs, and hope beats on. So must the works continue which "on that day" (a day known only to God, known only in hope by ourselves) will bring the blessing to fruition.

Meantime, we mourn and celebrate and keep on, some in prison, some outside. The works of peace and justice must continue to beat, like a fist against a wall of the adamant, to bring it down, a system of high and unaccountable crime.

No Savior but Yahweh (21:1–10)

21:1 Like a whirlwind
born of desert places
2 (this the sinister vision
granted me)
the spoilers set to pillaging
the destroyers to looting.
Save for Yahweh our savior
it were all up with us!

3 What sights, sounds, afflictions,
anguish of woman in childbirth!

4   My heart stopped in its tracks.
    . . . .
8   I long for the end of day—
    evening falls, pure terror.
9   My people threshed, ground under,
    leaven cast in the fire.

10 Yet
    Behold, from Yahweh Sabaoth,
    good news beyond imagining—

    cruel exile ended,
    the day, the hour of return!

The vision is affecting, all but overwhelming. Yet we have heard such proclamations before. On the face of it, in the face of contrary awful facts, the Isaian vision appears indefinitely delayed and increasingly unlikely of fulfillment. If so, it is hardly worth dwelling upon or praying for.

Truth told, it seems the visionary has gone mad. The boundary separating illusion from the "facts of the case," the brute "facts of life," has dissolved. What is to come, will be as is. Where you are, who you are, in what circumstance of sorrow or deprivation or anger or resignation: stop looking for change, embrace the system that is your plight, your destiny, even if it is the foreclosure of your humanity.

Thus would be the words of the contrary, imperial proclamation; the anti-gospel. Yet Isaiah and his like offer the bracing air of truth. Believe, penetrate awful events, hope against hope, pray to see!

This oracle and its ravishing news is taken up again in Revelation of John (14:8 and 18:2). Although in both Isaiah and John, the details of the downfall of Babylon are entirely wanting, the theme is the unexpected, abrupt demise of the mighty one. Final, and ironic, and against all human calculation—"Fallen, fallen is Babylon" (21:9).

Did the catastrophe issue from military mischance? Elsewhere the tradition is more explicit. The book of Daniel (chap. 5) relates that in the course of an orgy King Belshazzar was killed and the Persians invaded Babylon. Herodotus agrees.

The exact circumstances of the downfall, however, are hardly to the point of Isaiah or the Revelation. In the latter a great angel sounds the theme as abruptly as does Isaiah here. It is as though no outside assault was required. The empire had within itself the seeds of its destruction. Like its famed temple tower, the ziggurat of Marduk, the empire grew top-heavy and could no longer sustain the weight of foreign wars and domestic injustice and violence. And so it fell.

Babylon is the prototype of every empire. It is now a matter of archaeology, of digging and restoring in degree the noble ruins. But it is no more a living entity.

And what of Jerusalem? Jerusalem is sacked, the inhabitants captured. And yet . . . and yet, it cannot ultimately be removed.

Jerusalem may be pulverized and destroyed, but it ever rises from the rubble. What is more alive, more central today to the universal sense of the holy, whether of Muslims, Jews, Christians, than Jerusalem?

Land of No Vision (22:1–8)

22:1   Why this feverish
        untimely rejoicing—
    throngs on the housetops,
2   parades snaking by,
      flags, banners, slogans,
    cannon volleys
        all but extinguishing the sun?
        Banqueting and revelry:
        "Eat, drink!" they shout
        "for tomorrow we die!"
    I have news for you, sorry news.
    Those "sons of the fatherland"
    fell on no "field of honor,"
3   Your cause? tainted from the start.
        How could it not end badly?

    Death, death stalking the land!

death, arbiter, judge, usurper—

Hear me! Yahweh alone is God!
Malign revelers,
inconstant weathercocks!
this way, that, your hearts
reeling in mad winds!
ears itching, boots echoing
the throb of war drums—

4   Yahweh weeps.
Isaiah
keeps in his heart's vial,
the tears of God.

5   The holy city dissolves in darkness,
the warlike prevail!
the nation's heart grows vile—
panic, defeat, confusion.

Shout victory then
till the heavens shake
and the earth quakes—
you, the defeated victors!
. . . .
8   I name you anew.
No
you name yourselves—
Land of No Vision!

A profound emotional schizophrenia afflicts the nation. Can we call it unsuitable rejoicing, inappropriate to their plight? They rejoice when, in all sanity, they should be mourning.

A military spirit has set them, people and leaders alike, off kilter. National calamity is in the offing; everyone turns a blind eye. But the deeper, obscene, ultimately sorrowful meaning of the feverish frenzies is despair. They boldly cry out, "Let us eat and drink. . . ." Isaiah recognizes the despair. The vast majority do not.

If hope is a kind of seeing, a second sight or insight, despair is a blinding affliction. The connection with militarism is not to be missed. The armed forces are in motion; Jerusalem is being vastly fortified. The ecology within and without the city is being altered, insulted, from the waters of Gihon to the ancient reservoir of Shiloah, all in the effort to insure a water supply within the walls in case of siege.

In such ways, Hezekiah creates an obsessive national concentration of mind and muscle on war. Sennacherib has invaded the land; the holy city is threatened. As usual in wartime, a new religious atmosphere is engendered. God is declared either irrelevant to the main chance or is suddenly transformed into a partisan.

The first option seems to be the case here. Let us get on with the works of war, which war itself has made expedient, indeed crucial. Action is taken on two fronts—resisting the invader and fortifying the city. And after all, and before all (have we not heard this before—and will we not hear it again?), if ever there was a just war, surely it is this one!

Millennia after the Isaian events, would it not seem time at last to proclaim that war, just or unjust, declares God irrelevant?

This is exactly the message of Yahweh, who refuses to be silenced by the baying of the dogs of war, refuses in effect to be deemed irrelevant, "I your sovereign Lord, called you to weep and mourn, to shave your heads and don sackcloth" (Isa. 22:12).

An alternative is at hand, and what a strange alternative it is! It involves perhaps two implications: (1) Laying down arms, we confess our powerlessness. (2) So doing, we seek, in tears and mourning, the providence of God.

> Who then are the mourners? The mourners are those who have caught a glimpse of God's new day, who ache with all their being for that day's coming, and who break into tears when confronted with its absence.
>
> They are the ones who realize that in God's realm of peace, there is no one blind and who ache whenever they see someone unseeing. They are the ones who realize that in God's realm there is no one hungry and who ache whenever they see someone starving. They are the ones who realize that in God's realm there is no one falsely accused, and who ache whenever they see someone imprisoned unjustly. They are the ones who realize that in God's realm there is

no one who fails to see God, and who ache whenever they see someone unbelieving. They are the ones who realize that in God's realm there is no one who suffers oppression, and who ache whenever they see someone beat down. They are the ones who realize that in God's realm there is no one without dignity, and who ache whenever they see someone treated with indignity. They are the ones who realize that in God's realm of peace there is neither death nor tears and who ache whenever they see someone crying tears over death. The mourners are aching visionaries.

Such people Jesus blesses; he hails them, he praises them, he salutes them. And he gives them the promise that the new day for whose absence they ache will come. They will be comforted.

The Stoics of antiquity said: Be calm. Disengage yourself. Neither laugh nor weep. Jesus says: Be open to the wounds of the world. Mourn humanity's mourning, weep over humanity weeping, be wounded by humanity's wounds, be in agony over humanity's agony. But do so in the good cheer that a day of peace is coming.*

Balm in Gilead, Death no More (25:1–5, 6–8)

25:1   Yahweh, You are my God
      honor and praise be yours,
      Your holy design from of old!

2   The citadels of the proud
      You bring to ground, a rubble.

      . . . .

4   You, strength of the hapless,
      you, refuge of the poor.
      The violent wreak havoc!
      their reign—a torrid blast,
      a desert, a windborne plague

5   But you, you put to silence
      boasts of the hard of heart!

Isaiah opens with a prayer of thanksgiving on an exalted, but extremely realistic and concrete, note. Indeed, it is a strange sort of thanksgiving in that it takes into account most awful events, events that touch Isaiah's life as well.

*Nicholas Wolsterstorff, *Lament for a Son,* pp. 85–86, Wm. B. Eerdmans Publishing Co., copyright © 1987. Used by permission.

"You are my God . . ." (25:1). This revolutionary word is the clearing away of a dense forest of idols. It topples false gods, who in many lives, and as a plain matter of conduct, have been "my god" or "my gods."

The verse sings with a reasoned, clear-sighted ecstasy. God has put into the mouth of the prophet a flame of truth. The prophet cries out, knowing someone nears, a presence both wounding and healing.

For most mortals, this "You are my God" is indeed a leap into the dark. We neither see nor hear nor touch nor taste; the sense of God is neutral on our tongue and in our mind. Seldom or ever does the reality of God touch the heart. Our emotional life is, shall we say, drained away or directed elsewhere.

We give our hearts (hardly blamefully) to those we know and love—because we can see and hear and touch and kiss them.

So we plod along, more or less in the dark, more or less humiliated by the dreary quality of our prayer, our worship by turns inane and trivial, our sense of the holy vitiated, distracted, grown distempered. Preachers of an American pseudo-gospel and the tempests of a secular culture, by turns enticing and brutal, all but swamp us.

The toppling of the idols is not the work of benighted spirits like ourselves, who often as not cannot tell an idol from a burning bush. The toppling is the work of God, who knows, who loves. God, who is truth and love, immeasurable, clears a way in the underbrush, a way through our maze of faltering and waywardness, and offers us the Shekinah, leading us toward the holy sanctuary.

"You are my God." A child can say it; children do say it and sing it, content to use the simple words on their lips. Adults too, in the measure we are unbesotted by the world, utter a volume in this one monosyllabic phrase. It is a triumph, a gift from the One invoked. When many say it, heartfelt, we have the Plenary and Holy Twelve, and know "there I am in the midst."

How sorrowful that such words, and the joy and confidence they imply, are not as close to our affective life as a hand or an eye in motion are to our physical makeup.

Can we look on a lovely sky or tree or the sea and say it? Can we touch the face of a child and say it? In consequence of such beauty, touching it, touched by it, understanding (in the sense of standing under), we know the source of such beauty, the Resource.

I do not know if we can say this verse with a full heart, meaning it. Mostly we founder about with religious language, trying not to sound utterly absurd to ourselves and not invariably succeeding.

Witness the witless calling upon secular or military gods, the welter of special interests, the maneuvering for prideful place, the obsession with money and security. What we are left with is something else—the language of lapsed humans, the hiatus, the stammering, in a world that is "too much with us." God is absent, Unknown and unknowable (as we conclude in a kind of functional despair) and, for all that (with a shrug of dismissal), not counting for much.

But this is not all. In dire need of instructors, we have an instructor at hand whose counsel has endured. As we ruefully reflect, even a borrowed language is better than none. So we borrow and beg from the wise, if we would be less unwise.

We borrow from Isaiah. The God we invoke grants us a tongue to invoke. God is the builder and healer of the vacant and vapid and wounded mind. Left to its own devices (to our devices), it is dumb, blind, and deaf in the world. We, in truth, are no better than what we have made of that world. There remains the task of taking to ourselves the language of the great, the "seers"—like dwarfs in the armor of giants.

Thus the oracle at its very start, offers the plenary shock of a tradition brought to bear, bearing down. And yet it is strangely freeing as well.

Does there exist a "holy design" of things, a design sovereignly outside our wrecking will? We doubt it with all our crooked hearts. With doubt for a wrecking weapon, we set about proving the design is not so. Thus we remove ourselves from the unity, its beauty and truth and cherishing.

Or we set about proving (the same thing, only worse) that the design, whatever its shape or form, is in our hands, and in no others. It is we who create the world—even as we destroy it. Doubt becomes a habit of the mind, and the consequent wreckage—of truth, of community, of the world itself—follows close on.

I long to pay tribute to the design, to master the doubt, to enter that stream of life and holiness, that plan "formed of old." I want to believe I am called, beyond any doubt, beyond any wreckage of which I am capable—beyond a culture of doubt and wreckage.

Can one borrow a mood, a tone, a celebration, so foreign to the world, the way it goes? We are told that we can, that we must. The grand design exists, no matter what the world makes of it (or resolves to unmake).

The design of reality is nobly conceived by Isaiah. It is a web unfinished in the hands of a Weaver. Slowly the pattern of moral beauty and fidelity emerges. The Weaver summons us. We are free to weave and be woven or not. The web exists without us, does not require us. It stands firm, inviolate, anchored, and free.

And we? We can admire and bless and give thanks, or we can set about the work of wrecking. Thus the sorry tale of a wounded freedom.

Many choose to stand outside the design in a pitiful charade of the superhuman. They are free to be American, to be silent, to be complicit, to consume with ardor, to embrace violence like an iron bridegroom whose embrace is death.

And yet . . . and yet. The design of God, we are reminded, is "perfectly faithful." It perdures, no matter what, no matter the infidelity on our part. A majestic steadfastness reigns, an unstained love, for all the stains of our own venomous and adventuring generation.

The words of the prayer place us, willy-nilly, in a genetic line. Coming from somewhere, we may yet find our way—somewhere—through a mercy that greatly surpasses our sin.

"The citadel of the proud" has been brought down (25:2). It is a city no longer; it is rubble. What a gauntlet is hereby cast down! The statement is abrupt: it admits of no intervention, softening, or repair. What can it mean?

How scandalous is this Isaiah! The overthrow of the proud is adduced as the cause and occasion of holy praise. He proclaims "honor and praise be yours," for you have worked wonders and you have reduced the city to a heap of stones. What a strange juxtaposition of God's works! Equally strange: as the second statement evokes praise, so does the first.

In the beginning, as recounted in Genesis, the wonders of God were revealed majestically in days of creation. At the climax, humankind was placed in a garden of innocence. Then came a shadowy presence, a malice that whispers enticements, "You will be like God" (Gen. 3:5, NRSV).

So here, the report on the city is first of all a moral statement, a judgment of the state of human affairs here and now. It is the glance within, the conclusion of one whose moral glance pierces through semblances to the heart of matters. Judgment is mine, says God—here and now.

The outcome of moral crisis rests in other hands than the powers of this world. The nations will one day see. Pride and chariots and spears and all their military hardware and vaunting claptrap go—exactly nowhere. Is this salutary lesson perhaps the beginning of the end?

Then they will see that God is the God not of the big achievers and half-believers, but of the helpless, the needy, the victimized, the distressed (25:4 and 5). God is shelter and providential shadow. Such this God is for those who have no chariots to trust in.

Then there occur by way of contrast, powerful images of the once powerful, at length reduced and rendered, like a blast of rain against a wall, like intense heat in a time of drought. God brings their power to nothing, God comes like a cloud tempering a hot spot.

What can we make of all this? Certain forms of worldly power are excoriated here, held up to scorn. They are literally stuck, without hope or compassion. They never learn.

Isaiah offers (as do all the prophets) not only the judgment on the desperate measures of the old way, but also the possibility of a new way.

25:6 See, Yahweh prepares
on this holy mountain
a surpassing feast!
Only imagine—
for one and all
fat of the marrow,
ambrosial wines!
7 Here, on this mountain

God sweeps aside
the veil of sorrow,
the cloth of mourning—
8   death no more!
balm in Gilead!
heal-all upon every wound!

O day, we entreat, come soon!

The Grand Feast (v. 6) "for one and all" reflects the universal theme so dear to Isaiah and other prophets—Come, everyone; no one outside!

God plays host of the banquet. The feast is ready, the menu is dwelt upon with pride and anticipation. It is a menu for all, a serendipitous ethnic smorgasbord! Whatever delectables the people (all people) love, what awakens and satiates appetite, this will be served; "on this mountain," that is, Zion, the pivot of the universe, the place of ingathering and welcome.

So the end of things is to be a celebration. The image stands beyond phantasy or dream-wish. It is the substance of hope. The image is also exorcizing; it cleanses mind and heart, liberates us from images of technique, of destruction, annihilation, nuclear Armageddon.

God so loves creation! God would celebrate, and have us celebrate, not our mere perdurance or survival—let alone the utter destruction of all, as some have claimed (Armageddon being an idea whose time, so to speak, will never come). Here is a far different outcome; a universal banquet. God, together with the beloved people, will celebrate.

Celebrate what? The human is vindicated by the saints, by those who cherish creation. What was true in the beginning remains true through all the tormented path of history and is true to the end—God's love, our love, God-community, we in community, fair creation no longer "groaning, in travail" (Rom. 8:22). And a dance, a ring-around of creation, will follow the banquet, Christ calling the tune.

The tone changes in verses 7 and 8. It is as though the feast were proceeding as planned, in all splendor and pomp. Suddenly the overarching tent becomes strangely oppressive. A realization dawns, lies heavy on the spirit. We are not yet altogether liberated. There are empty places at table. Sorrow is in the air, a sense of loss, the absence of loved ones. At this late hour, when our liberation is announced and celebrated, is death yet in command?

Suppose that in the midst of the great feast the tent were to collapse. Not catastrophically, but it simply comes unmoored and wafts down slowly over the guests. It is silken, not suffocating, light as down. It falls and falls until it lies over the people, interferes with free movement, gets in the way of gesture and dance. It has become a kind of veil of mourning, a gauze, a caul. We no longer see each other clearly.

Are we the living? Are we the dead? We gaze at one another in wonderment and awe. Death has made its power known, even at the feast of life.

Something must be done. The guests cannot of themselves lift the veil, a tegument close as a second skin. It lays upon the living a symbolic claim. It says, "You do not know one another; but I know you. You may celebrate life as you please, but death owns you. Multitudes have died. You will all die. Eat, drink and be merry. . . ."

This is intolerable. The feast of life, given over to other, arrogant hands, becomes a feast of death!

The guests are helpless. Who shall lift the central pole, and with it, that huge adhesive burden?

God acts. Death is banished—forever.

Then, in a further ritual of tenderness, we see the God who welcomes, passing among the guests. They breathe freely once more, weep in joy and relief. God passes among them (surely this is the spontaneous tenderness of a woman) and wipes the tears from faces.

"God will remove the reproach from his people, over all the earth . . ." (25:8). This reproach contains all the forms, ploys, the callous, banal, splenetic ways and means of death, the terror of our history.

Appalled or numb, we hear with monotonous regularity of new attacks by the contras, civilian deaths high, or of the Salvadoran death squads, the witless bombing of Baghdad, the slaughter in Rwanda—likewise in the Philippines, in northern Ireland, in former Yugoslavia, in so many tormented regions of our world. At whose door will these crimes be laid? Who will requite the blood of the innocent?

These are very old questions, and, alas, ever and malevolently they are made new. They must be raised again and again, though the heavens turn to adamant and the skies rain blood.

"For God has spoken." This is the word of the awaited One, who is present, in hope. Thus meaning is bestowed on events otherwise opaque or absurd. Meaning is even bestowed on events that seem to have no meaning, that escape and evade and mock all possible meaning.

We have clear instruction concerning the character of this God who saves, God's moral physiognomy. The instruction is offered by Jesus in the Sermon on the Mount and is verified on the mount of Calvary. So clear is the message that it blinds. And, blind as midnight, we place our hope elsewhere, in almost anything, anyone— except God.

"From whom we hope for our salvation" (v. 9). There flourishes at large a hyper-spiritualized version of salvation. It is intensely concerned with self, with "rapture" (and the devil take the hindmost). Such salvation ferments, to all appearances, in the head only, a kind of pseudo-ecstasy, without cost or empathy or a sense of the suffering of the innocent. It is little concerned with our culture of death, or a critique of same, and much concerned with something known as the "afterlife."

So understood, salvation also welcomes, without critique or second thought, assimilation into mainstream America (a polluted stream, if ever one flowed), into cultural attitudes toward women, money, success, ego, and, perhaps above all, violence. Such salvation is purportedly apolitical. It is in fact hot with hellish politics. It acknowledges little or no difficulty with wars, hot or cold, with racism, violence, or foreign incursions.

Implied in this view is a quite clear conviction, a cultural one to be sure, that there is nothing seriously wrong with America. Quite the contrary, America is God's finest triumph. Let us wage wars, let us be racist and sexist and rampage over the earth; it is all blessed, all according to his [sic] will.

To be "saved" in this perverse sense is, in the final analysis, to have one's self, as sedulous child of the culture, justified by the gods of the culture. The Christians, the many whose Christianity dangles from the chief modifier, American, are justified in a wide swath of divine benignity.

There is another, more modest, thoughtful, critical understanding of salvation. In this view, the Christian is weaponless. Maybe he or she is disarmed, converted from former ways of violence. Such a one walks in the world burdened, at times overwhelmed, by a sense of sin and death. This one confesses, mourns, and seeks reconciliation. She or he crosses lines and enters forbidden territories, to declare the presence of the God of life in the midst of the lurking apparatus of death.

Such a one has little to boast of, either in one's own behavior or that of the culture. One hears from one's betters, the mystics, the hopeful word that "all will be well" and tries to believe it, if only because God has spoken—not (God knows!) because things are anything but grievously unwell.

From ill humor, rancor, dwelling perversely on the underside of things, deliver us, O God!

Isaiah has become the direct oracle of the divine will. Even now the rack and ruin are underway. We mourn, we rejoice, we endure.

Who Credits the Promises? (29:1–12, 13–24)

29:1 The years, the cycles—
    rite and ritual, ritual, rite.

2   Then
            this to come;
    the city
            besieged, surrounded,
    invaded.

3   Taken, sacked.
    The city called Holy
    a blood-drenched altar, end to end.

4   The city—
        a mouth stifled in dust.
    The city—
        a reedy conventicle of ghosts.

5   But patience, withstand!
     This too shall pass,
   the invaders fleeing,
       handful of straw, fine dust in a gale!
6   All those warriors, weapons,
     horses, banners,
   shouts—**Victory is ours**—
   torn, expunged from throat.
7   Victors?
   None.
8   Like the starving
     who dream of food and wake with gnawing guts.
     Like the thirsty, dreaming of water—
     they waken, mouth parched, a mirage.

9   Do my people credit the promise?

   You do not. Truth told,
         your bread is stupidity,
       your cup blindness,
10   spirits numb,
     prophets thrice blindfolded.
11   The word of Yahweh—
     a book thrice sealed.

Volcanic moods, irony, despisal, knowledge of betrayal, retribution are here. The people of faith and Yahweh, God of peace, have come to the crossroad here, in time and place.

The enemy is at the gates, a crucial moment indeed. Have the king and his advisers set their jaws? Must Israel ape the nations in the absolutely crucial respect of armed resistance? Armed resistance is the only hope, so goes the official line, backed by immense works of fortification and armed might confronting the invader.

Nothing of this will avail. The first part of the oracle is appallingly concrete. Despite all effort and ingenuity and expenditure, in 701 B.C.E. Jerusalem will be destroyed.

But this is not all (vv. 5–8). The prophet breathes deeply, and exhales on the reeking and ruinous air, a breath of hope. The occupation of the city will end, the barbarians will be routed.

> 29:13   Because, Because, Because
> I have plenary cause!
> Because this people offers lip service,
> because their fealty
> smells of convenience only—
> (see,
> the guile of their sages
> profitless, turgid
> an overripe fruit
> bursting in the hand)
> 14   And yet . . . yet . . . yet—
> despite all
> delicts, dereliction,
> I decree
> on their behalf
> patience, continuance,
> nay prodigal
> multiplications—
> like loaves, like fishes—
> of my prodigious deeds!

Here is a new mood of Yahweh, the astonishing One! The point is something like this—a desire to set human expectation on its head, especially that of the priests and highly placed counselors.

They reason in their (highly secular) skulls that they pursue the national interests according to their own understanding, utilizing their own ways and means. They invariably do not take into serious account the will of Yahweh or what passes for God's will according to Isaiah, the vocalist of the Holy One. Indeed, they ask, is it God's will or Isaiah's delusions? We have had to learn, alas, how to deal with this doomsayer. We face the harsh days and nights of invasion and the threat of the fall of Jerusalem. And his peremptory dicta forbid all armed resistance! Utterly absurd, if not ruinous.

If religion has a place here, it is to enforce with blessing and exhortation the national will. Let the priests stand firmly with the king and his counselors. Loyalty is the highest contribution of the religious sense, along with every other public structure, bent toward the resolution of this mortal crisis.

We simply do not know what this reliance on Yahweh could mean. Isaiah has not spelled out the matter to anyone's satisfaction. Are we to lay down our arms and, shortly thereafter, our lives? Are we to become yet another victim-vassal of this merciless enemy?

A messenger arrives; he bears word from the tyrant who threatens Jerusalem. Seldom has a bitter pill been so sweetly sugared! Do the people fear they will be herded into exile, to forced labor, to torture and death? Come now, by no means!

The message is couched in terms the people will resonate to. They ape the promise of Yahweh and speak of ancient symbols of salvation. Let the Jerusalemites know that their trust is misplaced; trust me, the emperor, my arms, my omnipotence:

> This is the message of the emperor of Assyria: "Make peace with me, hand yourselves over to me. And each of you will eat from his own fig tree and vine and drink from his own well. And I will come and lead you to a country much like your own, a land of wine and grain, of oil and honey. And you shall live and not die.
>
> (2 Kings 18:31–32)

After the velvet glove comes the fist uncovered. The threat is specific—greater force has always prevailed; the gods, including yours, are impotent before the engine of Armageddon. They are dead and we have buried them:

> Did the gods of any other nations save their countries from the emperor of Assyria? . . . Did anyone save Samaria? . . . When did the gods of any of those countries save their country from our emperor? Then what makes you think the Lord can save Jerusalem?
>
> (2 Kings 18:34–35)

The people take the bitter words to heart. Isaiah does not.
The king and people are summoned to forge their future in the

furnace of dire times, in an act of faith. You are not to know of this or that detail; you are to believe.

You are not to know; for, if you knew, the laying down of arms and the search for alternatives, bargaining, coming upon the moral equivalent of the threatened war—these would die aborning. No one who takes up arms searches out another way, a way other than the way of death.

Therefore the promise must remain just that—a promise. Your reliance on the promise is in effect your act of faith.

Is it absurd to believe, utterly and as a matter of social decision, to forbid yourselves all recourse to the logic of the world, war in response to war? Even if the armed enemy is battering at the gate? Is the refusal to be censured by the logicians of this world absurd? If so, let it be so.

We stand with Isaiah, who stands with Yahweh.

When the king hears the message of the envoy, his wits are scattered. Utter despair, moral disarray master him. He posts his envoys to the prophet. The message is like a long, drawn-out whining:

2 Kings 19:3   Day of opprobrium
of shame, confusion.
A woman comes to term
weak, distraught—
no strength
to push the unborn into the world!

4   You Isaiah
hear (Yahweh hears!)
the mick-mockery, the dudgeon
of vaunters at the gate

Send a prayer heavenward
in favor of the few, how few
(and who, mayhap God knows)—
might this day survive!

The response of Isaiah has an utterly different tone; it is brief, to the point, filled with the confidence of a believing heart:

6 Fear not!
7 I will weave about your enemy
a fine filament of rumor.
holding him close

as a child's hand a father's,
whirling him round and about
this way, that, at My sweet will, until
a watchword dims his wits;
Depart!
And he departs.

(2 Kings 19:6–7)

We find it difficult to unravel this extremely complex ruler Hezekiah with whom Isaiah had to deal. Not all the reports in 2 Kings are dim. His chief claim to fame seems to have arisen from his relentless suppression of idolatry. Indeed, in summing up his reign, the chronicler grants Hezekiah the sanctified formula bestowed only on just rulers, from David onward; "He did what was pleasing to the Lord" (2 Kings 18:3). And more, the praises mount, even to the point of extravagance: "Judah never had another king like him, either before or after his time" (18:5). Yet again: "He was faithful to the Lord, and never disobeyed Him. . . . So the Lord was with him, and he was successful in all that he did" (18:6–7).

It is as though several historians assembled the stories, perhaps from different sources, evidently without concern for consistency. One is content to eulogize; another takes a dim view. In one scene Hezekiah grovels before the might of Sennacherib the Assyrian. He accuses himself of wrongdoing, elsewhere unexplained. He then proceeds to an enormity of appeasement; he strips the temple and palace treasury of gold and silver, and ships the loot off to the foreign despot.

29:15 Damnable
the lurkers in dark corners!
adroit, double-minded,
concealing from all save Me
shameful machinations!

16 Is the potter naught but his clay?
    Does the pot boast
    to the cunning hands
    that fashioned it close,
round and round
to utmost perfection;
"Self-made am I?"
Rebellious ones,
Race of great liars—
You say to the prophets
"No more, those unpalatable
truths of yours!
No, deck us in royal
flattery, cope us
heel to crown
in fine spun
illusion.

Send us forth
to dead ends,
to detours and mazes!"

Isaiah, write it down;
conceal the scroll
in a blind cave
that the blind may not see,
the deaf hear not.

17 And then, and then
    in no very great
    time to come
    but soon and sooner—
18 the deaf shall hearken to
    sacred sibilants,
    from night's dense shadow
    the blind shall issue!

The image of the pot in the hands of the potter is an ancient one that urges a certain truth of existence. In this case, our fragility, dependence, our place in the scheme of creation is hinted at only by this analogy. Yahweh, in transcendence, draws humans into existence from all but nothing—the clay, the dense earth.

The exchange between potter and pot is lightheartedly dramatic. The image is drawn again and again; by Isaiah (45:9; 64:8), by Jeremiah (18:1–6; 19:1–13), and finally by Paul (Rom. 9:20–21). It seems as though the Bible cannot have too much of exploring this scene, the human again and again self-endangered by Promethean pride, yet even ridiculous in such pretension!

In contemporary terms, if some "advance" in technology (from the technology of war to the technology of medicine and biology and everything between) is feasible, then we say, Let us proceed—and moral considerations be ever so gently damned.

Dare the clay, the pot, talk back to the potter? Dare it abandon the truth of its nature in favor of the image of the "self-made pot"? The absurdity of the pot grown vocal, the human grown manifestly proud, is obvious. No comment is required. Good-humored Isaiah!

Alas for You: Haste, Waste, Misapprehension (30:1–18, 19–26)

Delegations have been dispatched to Egypt, perhaps by order of Hezekiah. Isaiah is infuriated; he launches a philippic against behavior he considers chicanery and betrayal.

30:1   Cursed be the rebellious,
       devious plans in place,
       crime upon crime!
  2   This plan, that pact,
       security here, advantage there!
  3   Hear this;
          your intrigues—
       a hall of mirrors, illusion
       upon illusion.
          Do you scheme?
       shame, you trespass
       in a house of horrors,

8   Write this down, Isaiah
          Seal it close,
               My words languish, lost, dead
     by a dead sea,
               unseen, unheeded—
          the blind, begetting
          blind generations to come.
     Seal the cave mouth,
     roll across
     a great boulder,
          all in silence, as though
          undersea!
12 This people—
          to what
          compare them?
13   a firm-seeming wall
          a mortal crack runs through.
          It sways, it heaves and buckles
          and falls asunder!

14   This people—clay,
          a pot of faulted clay—
          shattered.
               Shards
          useless at the hearth,
          worthless at the well!
15 Hearken to me, my people!
          peace be your dwelling,
     trust, your refuge!
16   But no.
     Like a steed at the starting gate
               impatient, impassioned
               you shudder—
                    Let us be off!
          Very well then,
          unpeaceable, distrustful ones!

          Hear what comes of this

haste, waste, misapprehension—

nothing, and less—
catastrophe, defeat.

Let rumors converge,
17   thousands will flee.
Let the sun assert
sovereignty at dawn—
your armies dissolve
like mist in midair!
Look what is left to you;
    a tattered pennant
    on a hilltop hanging
    like a hanged
    head, disconsolate—
    in stale air stalemated
    signifying
    nothing.

18   And yet
    despite all—
    mine, my people!

Write this, Isaiah;
"I condemn you to—
hope!"

This is the great refusal, the "original sin"—the nations, including Isaiah's own, abandon the faith in favor of military power and polity. But the prophet cannot not believe it. He has experienced the holiness of Yahweh; his exhortations to the powerful follow on the crucial moment when Yahweh revealed who he is. Such a revelation could not but collide with the powers of the world.

Turn to Yahweh, you worldly ones! Abandon arms and duplicity! The wisdom of Yahweh then will be manifest in your favor, infinitely surpassing in spirit, tactic and outcome, your tawdry diplomacy, your feverish selfishness and violence.

Alas, the word goes by the board; the wars and incursions continue. So judgment comes, the destruction of Judah, the reduction of the people to vassalage for more than a generation. So "the king of Assyria deported the Israelites into Assyria" (2 Kings 18:11). The rod of God's anger had done its work.

After anger, consolation. National and personal humiliation is not the last word. The word to the exiles is verdant with hope:

30:19　One day, my people—
　　　　one Day you will weep no more.
　20　No more the bread of agony, the waters of distress.
　　　　The holy One will hearken, answer you.
　21　Though you wander from the right path, you will hear;
　　　　this the way,
　　　　follow it close!
　22　You will cast down your idols of silver and gold,
　　　　those unclean nothings.
　23　That Day, I send abundant rain for planting and gleaning;
　　　　your harvests, nourishing, succulent.
　　　　. . . . . . .
　26　That Day; the moon will stand bright as a sun.
　　　　And the sun? seven times its light upon you,
　　　　the light of seven days upon you!
　　　　My Day and yours;
　　　　Yahweh succoring, binding up wounds;
　　　　wounds of God's people—of God's own heart.

Yet, this promise cannot be taken literally because the post-exilic condition of the survivors was shabby and poverty stricken. So the glory, here symbolized in benign and abundant nature, will arrive only at the end time.

Sword of the Spirit (31:1–9)

31:1　To seek protection
　　　　from violent hands—
　　　　　death!
　2　Egregious betrayers—
　　　　I plead time and again;

　　　　return to me!
3　　　Those "allies" of yours—
　　storehouses, treasuries, luxury, panoply,
　　　　borders bristling, chariots, shields
　　　　　warriors at the ready—
　　　　　　are these then gods?
4　　　　Hearken to me;
　　　your steeds are of bone and sinew, not spirit—
　　　　your soldiers mere homunculi.
　　　Weapons I strike from their hands,
　　　　armies I tumble in the sea!

　．　．　．　．　．　．　．

9　　　Your standard I snatch away,
　　　hold it aloft in mockery, trample it under!
　　see, I forge, unsheathe, brandish
　　　　the sword of the spirit!

Time and again the summons to nonviolence is sounded by the invoking of consequence, violence begetting its like, or its worse. Nonviolence is proclaimed as a social and political necessity, by no means limited to a matter of personal behavior.

Yet the society most nearly bound to the biblical summons today is the church. The church is not to be bound to the violence of the politics of empire nor to be a proponent of "just-war theory" nor of an economic order that inevitably tends in the direction of war, itching for its spoils.

The church must counter a theory of the human that implies, no avers, that violence is to be taken for granted as genetic structure. We cannot overlook the larger inevitable conclusion—macho personal conduct is the perfectly accoutered potential and boot camp of the warrior spoiling for a fight.

The church proclaims the alternative, stands in opposition to the just war. Nor can it condone other personal and social behavior short of war. We are what we include. The human grasp stops short of the inhuman weapon, spurns it or lays it aside.

Thus, the anthropology and self-command of the early "novus homo," the human reborn, was announced in the early years of the church.

Let the state and statecrafters "go down to Egypt" (31:1). That is the game of betrayal, not only of the God of peace, but also of their own people.

Let there be something else, a community capable of sounding a moral no, loud and clear. In the academy they call it a community capable of an "ethic of virtue." Let that community in steadfast resistance offer a traditional, biblical version of the human.

Let this version stand in courage, over against the splenetic, grasping, itchy, warrior-at-the-ready, finger-on-the-bomb version peddled by the collaborationists.

In fine, let there exist an Isaian community, faithful to his version of the human, animated by his spirit. Imagine the all but unimaginable—such folk as are apt to take Isaiah (and his God) seriously!

4
War:
Hearts and Minds Deranged

In view of the current domestic landscape of relentless, apparently triumphant high crime, Isaiah is consoling and reassuring. The reality of God's judgment lends dignity and seriousness to moral actions.

Yahweh, Our Hope Is in You (33:1–6, 7–16)

33:1   Destroyers
    intact and strong—
    ravenous your pillage and piracies!
    End, a sorry end for you.
    Ravening, pillage, piracy—
    you at long last the victim!
  2   Pity, Yahweh, we pray—
    our hope in you,
    our strong arm,
    dawn of full day
    our refuge in distress.

    . . . .

  6   Knowledge of you
    be our chief treasure!

We note two implications here. First, ample time and space are granted evildoers. Second, crime, biblically understood, is imputed time and again to those in power. This is the bias of the God whose view of history and of power is invariably "from below."

The advantage in the present, according to Isaiah, inevitably belongs to the powerful. The wicked have in their favor, tactically speaking, the refusal of the faithful to use their methods. The wicked then cannot summon the excuse that they are only "responding in kind." Nothing of the tactic they have used on others has been their own fate; they act in a kind of void of malevolence. They exercise evil, killing, control, for the pure hell of it; which is to say, for the ego of it.

Nevertheless, judgment is inescapable. It is in the nature of God, who is a God of justice. God in justice (holiness) created and so endowed us with God's own passion for "fair play, fair share" access to power, protection, and vindication in the human drama.

Alas, this primordial endowment, this patrimony (matrimony) of ours has been squandered. The loss of a sense of justice, and the consequent dismantling or degradation of structures of justice, are according to Paul, the primary sense and meaning of sin (see Romans 4 and 5). It is lost to the degree that restoration (redemption) must be considered an act of God, never of ourselves. We are by nature unjust, that is, but for God's mercy, we dwell so far from the justice of God as to be children of wrath.

Power indeed corrupts. No one of us, left to our own devices and designs, but would be found in the ranks of the treacherous and the destroyers. This statement offers a sobering anthropology. It is not to be understood as a datum of psychology or a sorry summation of history (it is also these), but it is a revealed truth of scripture. Self-exempted from the judgment of God, human activity is inevitably debased. Selfishness and the rule of the jungle prevail.

Anyone dealing perforce with justice systems learns much of structural sin. Whether one considers law courts, jail conditions, treatment of prisoners, or whatever, the inability of such institutions to approach their own ideal or match their rhetoric is a fact both plain and lamentable.

My brother and friends, and myself to a degree, have had ample experience over the years with the principalities and powers. Philip and three friends were tried and convicted in the courts of North Carolina because they had dared enter the notorious Seymour-Johnson Air Base and pour blood and work symbolic damage with hammers on an F-2 bomber.

The behavior of judge and prosecutors betrayed their contempt or willful ignorance, or both, toward the law, the defendants, the media, the church. They refused to hear testimony about the reason for the action, as a protest against mass murder wrought by the American air force from the bombing of Hiroshima to the carpet bombing of Hanoi to the smart bombing of Baghdad. The defendants were prepared to offer expert testimony touching on several germane points—international law, the crimes of the air force, United States foreign policy, conscience, the necessity defense. Such testimony was all gaveled out of order. The defendants were summarily disposed of in the manner of rapists or robbers. The perversion of justice continues.

With verse 2, we enter a far different scene. Tables are turned; the lowly and holy take part in judging the wicked. A prayer of candor follows, a direct plea for help: "Our strong arm, dawn of full day, our refuge in distress." Our needs are never done with. The need and the prayer, both become a rhythm of life itself.

One thinks of the difficulty of starting anew each day. One is haunted by a conviction that one's work will never be finished as long as life lasts—never to see the end, never to see peace in the world, peace in the cities, peace in homes and marriages, in the marketplace. What one sees one undoubtedly will continue to see into the indefinite future. The conditions that made of life one long cry for justice go on and on in spite of all persevering effort.

The morning prayer day after day, year after year, makes the long haul bearable. Life, and the work that gives life a human face, must be renewed, started over, again and yet again.

One thinks of the morning prayer of Dorothy Day, of Thomas Merton, and of so many others who were meticulously, stubbornly faithful to the tasks appointed. The matters they petitioned and worked for were hardly granted in their lifetime. They died without seeing the fruit of their prayer. But this was not the point. Their prayer was not a ransom note nor a final offer nor a demand for unconditional victory. They were not peddling magic. They did not demand an answer, a solution, an end, visible, palpably due them, to war or poverty or wrong-headed power. They worked, they prayed, they went on. For all the darkness around and within, they refused to give up. Their prayer had no codicil, no "or else."

They did not pray in order to play god before God but to play human before God. They submitted to an awful world of war and despair, alienation, injustice, bigotry, felonious power—our world. Their submission, their not giving up, was (and is) a kind of death. To pray, as they knew so well, is to taste death, to let go, cut loose. The world is in better hands than ours even though it is also in our hands.

The prayer does not depend on the answer to prayer, the answer not being in our keeping or ken. The answer does not follow in the sense of ineluctable cause and effect nor a guarantee attached to a product. We pray, knowing and not knowing.

We know, if we know anything, that we are not allowed not to pray. Now and again we sense in an obscure way that our prayer is hearkened to by Someone most loving. We come to realize that prayer is simply an activity of those who would be human. Prayer befits and honors the human, as does breathing, eating, loving, rejoicing, mourning.

Invariably, I dare say, especially in the experience of great and holy spirits, the effect of such prayer of the morning is simply that life goes on; the effort goes on. Perseverance is the only answer. There is nothing spectacular, no breakthrough. But for all that, prayer will not be silenced, even by the silence of God.

One thinks also of the millennia of prayer that link our morning prayer to the time of Isaiah and before. The beat goes on. We have great ancestry, holy rabbis, teachers. Shall we have descendants to match them?

In verse 3 the theme of judgment continues. While judgment is welcomed and longed for and seen as a welcome vindication by the just, a clearing of the air, it is seen by the evildoers only as an interference in the normal functioning of things, as indeed it is. The mood of God darkens to a threat; God here shows the other terrifying side of love.

The mighty agglomerates of self-interest the Bible calls "principalities" continually break up, then clot in new forms (yet always the same forms). Assyria rises, then Babylon, Egypt, and Rome; and Israel is continually tempted to ape the mighty neighbors. They find both strength and sense in a kind of cohesion of evil. The atmosphere is one of willed ignorance of moral disorder and a willed conspiracy of method and means.

Thus, for example, are the courts today, exemplified in the Plowshares trials. Jailing the peacemakers, they act not as instruments of justice but simply as juridical enforcers of corrupt governmental policy. In this egregious miscarriage, it should be added, an inert citizenry is complicit.

The scattering of the nations is a sign of God's abandonment of the entire vile enterprise. The situation of the nations often comes down to this: the methods adopted—the sword taken up, the invasions and seizures—simply do not work. Things fall apart. The evildoers cannot hang together. The lies self-destruct, the liars self contradict. This is our consolation, sorry and meager though it be.

Yet such consequences are tardy, always tardy. In Salvador a web of bestial cruelty was woven over a decade. Peasants and priests and nuns and workers were caught in the toils, and thousands perished. For all those hideous years, all this was denied; no one in authority knew anything and all allegations were ridiculed and denied, whether in Washington or San Salvador.

Meantime, the death squad leaders were being quietly trained in Fort Bragg, North Carolina. Their curriculum included modes of torture. The latest arms were supplied them. An agreement was implicitly reached: against adversaries real or supposed, they could move exactly as they wished, whether the enemy was an archbishop, Jesuits, nuns, or catechists.

A crude and telling image is presented in verse 4. The nations resemble, not the noble beasts they adopt for emblems—bulls, eagles, lions—but creatures of far less beauty, caterpillars and locusts. They gather spoils, they rush about. The sense is one of uncontrolled appetite, mindless, incoherent, and fretful.

The fictions of the powerful—"rational discourse," "sensible action," "measured response"—all are revealed for what they are, a joke and little more, inevitably sorry and costly to others. Revelation of the tawdriness and self-interest that mar "high-level decisions" is a work of God also. We Christians must literally make light of these lightweights in high places, posing foolishly as they do, huckstering like discredited Joves their images of omniscience and omnicompetence. A laugh at their expense saves much. It echoes the millennial smile on the face of the Buddha.

One could laugh long and hard, pass one's whole life in a laughing mood, were the high and mighty the only victims of their own pratfalls. Alas, they are not. The fate of their victims brings a chill to the heart.

Still we are heartened by these wondrously deflating images of the great ones under the gaze of God. Their behavior is appetitive, blind, wayward; they are caterpillars, locusts. They pile up their booty and spoils. They rush about frantically, evaluating, toting up, investing, trading, pirating about the world. Having stolen a great heap of booty, the thieves are bewildered about how to divide the spoils. In mind they hurry about, weighing alternatives. Who is to be trusted? Must we now mount a guard night and day against the implied threat of fellow freebooters? Has the game of cops and robbers been wonderfully reversed, the robbers perforce having become their own cops?

Verse 5 offers a continuing relief. The judgment goes on, a counterpoint to the dissonance of the lawless. "The Lord reigns on high," again the image of Yahweh as someone "from on high." God, we are told in another place, stepped down. We are grateful beyond words for this new image; a God who chose a place "on low." And on the first Good Friday of our sorry world, in a weary procession of shame from court to court, God's Son illustrated in his own torment the incivility and injustice of the powers. After a sorry judicial charade, the one from below died at the hands of the powers.

Only then was he "raised on high" (see Phil. 2:9). The logic opens, like a bronze hinge a mighty door, slowly, portentously, revealing what lies within. The mystery that is Christ stands revealed.

No cheap grace is granted, even to him. Exaltation, vindication; but first, death.

"Knowledge of you be our chief treasure" (v. 6). God is our stability, but God is also, be it noted, the unsettler of times and seasons and entire peoples. The phrase "fear of God," translated here as a "treasure," is of point. We are required to fear God. But one need have no fear of a God who again and again, like the nod of a metronome, signals a go-ahead to the latest spasm of violence. One would do well to fear the God who signals sternly: "No more of this."

33:7 Alas, for witness of my word
      vile recompense—
      scorn, hatred, defiance,

   8 the holy covenant reneged on,
      the scripture
      flung to four winds—this
      "dead letter"—this
      "matter of no moment."

   9 See now; the land trembles,
      blasphemous hands set ablaze
      a temperate
      flourishing zone.

      Conquest!
      sterility and waste;
      they make a desert,
      they call it—peace.

  10 I name it death.
      I score the word deep, deep
      on the barred postern: death.
      In the ruined garden: death.
      On the tempestuous
      brow of warriors: death.

  11 A rubble, a ruin, your works—
      straw, chaff in a storm!
      . . . .

  14 Who then holds firm, who
      honors my sovereign word?

  15 Let her stand forth, the just one
      in realms of darkness
      she burns gemlike,

her face
in joy and travail
      mirroring my own!

Things are at a sorry pass. The description ranges far; Isaiah insists that no sin is an island, none without consequence. One can choose to declare "my sin is my own affair." But this declaration is bound to be challenged. That sin invariably amounts to a form of betrayal, a violation of covenant, is an all but obsessive theme and image of the prophets. Consequent on betrayal of the sworn word, the consequence overflows into nature, a falling away of fruitfulness and beauty, the pollution of fair earth.

In verse 10 the breakthrough takes a quite unexpected (and hardly welcome) form—God as fire! God's response is kindled amid the chaff and stubble to which an entire people has been reduced by their own choices.

They have conceived chaff, useless fantasy, blown about on every wind. (What more powerful image of a people at the mercy of media that invade mind and heart to scatter, distract, and discredit the human!) Thus the people are reduced to a kind of stubble, cut down, all but level with the ground, pitiful and scant. The scattered grains left after the real harvest is gathered are hardly worth the trouble of the gleaners.

"Who then holds firm, who honors my sovereign word?" There is a supposition here—judgment is already underway.

Here and now, judgment, accountability?

We want no such thing. We prefer, all said, the merciless, less than human drama of anything goes. Not of course, spectacular crime, but something like moral numbing, adjustment to the world and its implacable and devious ways. Thus does the world lay claim to communities and bend them to its own crooked image.

In contrast, the "just one" stands forth. One thinks of Dante's *Purgatorio,* especially of the canto describing the healing of lust. The repentant dance in the fiery knot of judgment. And in the dance, they come upon a great mercy.

To judge, be it insisted, is not to condemn.

To judge is not to condone.

To judge is to announce God the merciful, not God the neutral.

To be judged is not to be condemned.

To be judged is not to be condoned.

To be judged is to undergo God the merciful, not God the neutral.

Finally, to be judged is to hearken and submit to the voice of community. Thus judgment is rendered active and merciful, both an acceptance and an invitation to conversion.

We are offered, in verse 15, the enduring qualities of the one who stands in the fire of judgment. This ideal human is not merely an ideal. She exists; she is human. She is, moreover, commended to us by a human named Isaiah (see also Ps. 15 and Ps. 24:3–5). The limitation of the human is conceded. Indeed, when ideal women or men are presented in the Bible, they are not presented as static portraits. There is no cult of personality here.

Thus when Mary utters her Magnificat (Luke 1:46), she does not commend virtuous conduct, her own or that of other mortals. The weight and import are elsewhere. It is the works of God in history that raise her spirit, especially those works, properly godlike, that "exalt the lowly, and overthrow the arrogant" (Luke 1:52).

There is difference between the Magnificat and the ideal human in Isaiah. The woman Mary is no abstract ideal but a vessel brimming with life. Her God brings social upheaval. She nurtures and so works wonders. (Consider God in the image of woman, God the nurturer who works wonders.)

Isaiah's ideal one is, of course, depicted in masculine language for the most part. The question here could perhaps be put: What does a man look like, presuming he is both just and under judgment? What works strike us as godlike?

Some of the works presented as ideal are traditionally male works, evidences of manly virtue. Public virtue is praised. The virtues presuppose a society in which men are in charge of money and offices. Such a one "rejects unjust gain . . . takes no bribes. . . ." This view seeks to preserve a superior ethic within a settled social arrangement. The presumption is that the system itself is inherently sound. One works to better it.

The other view, that of the woman, is fluid, open to the winds, charismatic, impatient with the idea that one should breathe life into a system it judges to be moribund. The woman's question would seem to be, What are the works of God that exalt one to a peak of song and celebration? Mary is uninterested in ethical ideals or icons. She is a great listener in the world, attentive to the tradition. She draws quite naturally on the words and images of others whose rhythms are one with her own.

Hence, the song of Mary draws on Anna, Habakkuk, Psalms, and, repeatedly, Job and Isaiah. She summons God the feminine, in whose image she is created, God the wild and untamable and impatient, the one who shakes women into motion, into fury, into new understanding of self and the world.

This is the God she celebrates! Such a God is furious before a world in which an inhuman system rules with a rod of iron, rules over women and children and men alike, allocates or withholds resources, dominates, legislates, is alert to the interests and prospering of the high and mighty. Such a system misuses and insults and derides the powerless. No more of this, she cries.

Her God gives life, exalts the lowly, overturns thrones, feeds the hungry, turns the proud to dust.

There is subtlety here, indirection, a theme emerging, a history in the making. According to Mary's ecstatic poem, a new woman is about to be born. Great music is in the air. The human is rejoiced in and celebrated. The works of God pluck Mary from anonymity and place her at the side of the great ones of history.

This God justifies her also, shamed as she is in the eyes of an inhuman law. The Holy Spirit fathers her child. She stands there, to do in her own time and dwelling the great work, indeed the greatest.

The just one imagined by Isaiah is holy and ecologically sensitive and touches reality at every point. Justice is seen as a kind of firm footing, then a growth, a flourishing of moral grandeur. The just one is fed by the world he (she) hungers for, thirsts for, welcomes, and cherishes.

Swords, Your Might and Vaunt (34:1–17)

34:1   Listen to me, worldlings!
       amassing riches,
       trafficking in violence—
       listen to my word!
         I speak of outcomes, befallings—

assured, awful beyond imagining!
3   In your nostrils the stench of corpses,
mountains ruddied with blood,
the skies rolled up, a parchment,
stars like leaves of autumn
wind driven, fallen to earth—
rivers afire, hearths quenched.
4   Your mad presumption
the storming of heaven—

5–6   Furies pursue you!
Swords, your might and vaunt,
drawn—at your throat!

7   And you—
slain like beasts of sacrifice
reeking upon the altars, you
heaped there, a hecatomb!

8–10   Forever and ever, the burning!
In your proud cities
no human footfall,
no vestige even, no echo
sweet voiced, of children.

11–15   Jackals preying, sleepless ravens,
vultures, vipers on the prowl.

Foreclosed, foresworn the human.
Law and order your vaunt?
No; chaos—
ghosts, demons, satyrs
coupling, encamping
the corridors of darkness.

16–17   Behold—my beloved, my creation
a mutilated scroll!

The world
I give over.
    Yours the making,
O unmakers.
    Enter
and be damned
the anteroom of hell!

What we mortals make of creation!

There is an end of patience, even of the patience of God. There can be no more awful judgment than this, no more awful images of moral darkness and the demonic, in all Scripture.

The oracle is launched, we note, with utmost confusion of spirit, in face of seeming prosperity. The realm is flourishing, yet Isaiah is hardly fooled. The rake is revealing himself in the very rake's progress. Behavior is consequential; judgment is built into the moral fabric of the universe. The glance of the prophet pierces the flush of appearances; he sees the violence, greed, and moral disarray boiling away just beneath the surface of things, smart and smooth as these seem.

Moreover, in the understanding of the great bard, nature becomes the revealer of nature. No creature is blind, he avers. No phenomenon is a dead end. Each leads beyond itself—even the ghosts and haunts that prowl our dreams and reveal to us or conceal from us that our moral darkness is hardly uninhabited.

Every human life, every institution is a field of combat in which death and life, faith and faithlessness contend. When humans renounce human behavior in favor and servitude to whatever appetite, the soul (world soul, my soul) is not merely emptied of human capacity. It is possessed by the inhuman, by the spirit and force and utmost prevalence of the power of death. The ruins become a cote for preying beasts and birds.

The awful judgment is itself a mercy. And mercy, not judgment stark and unmodified, has the final say.

Turn, Turn About: To Homeland, to Self, to Sanity
(35:1–10)

35:1– 2   Let the arid land
breathe free,
sweet respiration, rain!
Let the steppes cry out
(winterlocked, beyond
the warmhearted sun's
midday ministration)
    in bird song, song of flowers,
    spring's freehold, winter's
    yielding at last
        cry—Life!
    evermore, abundant—Life!
    And the Giver of Life, a glory
    half glimpsed, the bridegroom
    at the portal lingering—
    our strength, our passionate One!
    His shadow falls, pure light.

You, the sorrowful, glean
from that glance of his, hope's
first faint inkling, then
strong and stronger!

3–4   See!
hands impaired, aged,
at merest touch of his
    flex and flow—graceful grow,
    apt to appointed tasks!
    And the sagging knees
    the spines bent double
    (unremitting the heft
as on beasts of burden laid)
straight, upright sprung,
aside once for all
cast
their slavish estate!

5   Come blind, come deaf—
      sit at the undreamed
      banquet of sound and sense!
      loosened the tongue
      to praiseworth, to song!

8–10   Speedy our homecoming!
      The way like a royal
      tapestry, the Via Regis
      close-woven of creation—

      we ransomed, we exiles
      leaping, dancing for joy!

It is as though the wickedness of worldly events were a mirage, as though judgment were finally dissolved in mercy. The prophet's final word, when all else is said, all darkness taken into account, celebrates the goodness of creation under the benign gaze of Yahweh.

All things are restored and reconciled! Attend to the promise! Its utterance, its fullness, its fidelity and sure realization break the heart. Isaiah has come through it all—slavery, humiliation, scorn, exile. Even so, his people have come through, purified and restored. They have survived not only a weak and vacillating king, wrong turns, bad polity, and the poison of public violence endorsed by themselves but also wars and rumors of war.

They have survived the wrath of Yahweh, unleashed again and again on their heads by the fierce prophet in their midst. They have survived—Isaiah.

The heart of this great one, this recalcitrant amanuensis of the Holy, this unyielding one, this stone in the path of empire, the one who must be silenced and dismissed and scorned and finally disposed of!

Yet his heart is like a full vessel, immeasurably enlarged, wide as the world to contain and convey the hope of generations. His heart overflowing in joy, he composes a very ode to joy!

What, we muse, were the circumstances of his joy? Was he still in favor in the court of Hezekiah? Was the king (on occasion, for the time being) granting him a hearing, even seeking him out for a clue, a word from on high? Or was Isaiah already banished and unheard from? Is this (a wilder speculation) his swan song, composed just before his execution?

You Great Ones: Dust in God's Hand
(37:22–29; 38:10–20)

37:22   Who is it, then,
        you dare blaspheme against?
        It is I, the Holy One!

23   Your vaunts offend my ears!
24   "Our weaponry! Our stores of gold!
        We level the Himalayas,
        nothing immune to our might.
    Every horizon ranged,
    drawn within our scope.
    "We shape and shake creation,
    enter where power appoints,
    lay claim at sweet will.
25   Euphoric, we drink at wells
    mirageous, half-heard of.
    Under our thunderous footfalls
    great rivers grow tame, recede
    like caged lions, cornered!"

26   Empty vaunts, words, words!
    Rush hither and yon, catastrophic ones
    subdue, enslave, slaughter as you will!
    I aver, I stipulate.
27   It is I who permit
    outrageous
    puny godlings
    to draw breath in the world
28   Not an arrow launched
    but I appoint direction—
    true it strikes, or wide the mark.

29   Judgment then!
     you broken, roped, in harness
     a ring in your nose,
     a dumb ox drawing
     waters of grace
     from a well unfailing—
         you,
         a snatch
         of grass of the field—
         my anger blows hot;
         you, dry dust in my hand.

There can be no more terrifying indictment of a species of power unbridled by conscience than this charge levied against Sennacherib, king of Assyria, who had laid siege to Jerusalem. In fear Hezekiah prayed for deliverance, and Isaiah responded with this judgment from God. What then happened is a question that has been the subject of endless probing into the records and remains. Why did Sennacherib's army turn back at the cusp of victory as they stood before Jerusalem? Someone, something smote hard: "That night, an angel of the Lord went to the Assyrian camp and killed 185,000 soldiers. At dawn next day, there they lay, all dead. Then the Assyrian emperor withdrew and returned to Nineveh" (2 Kings 19:35–36).

There is a consensus of sorts that a plague broke out among the besiegers (the number of casualties being grandly inflated by popular report). In any case, the ceaseless insistence of Isaiah (no arms, no foreign entanglements) was vindicated, though tardily and with great pain on all sides.

It is a pity we are not offered an inkling of the practicalities that would translate Isaiah's counsel of reliance on Yahweh into action. Again and again, Isaiah reassures and shores up the vacillating king: "The Lord tells you not to let the Assyrians frighten you with their claims that God cannot save you." The promise of an intervention was a rather weak one, it must be admitted, in view of other versions of events. What indeed followed on his prediction was this: "The Lord will cause the emperor to hear a rumor that will make him go back to his own country . . ." (2 Kings 19:5–7).

Was the plague striking down the Assyrian forces to be thought the solution? In the meantime, were the people so paralyzed as to remain passive, merely awaiting, on the word of Isaiah, a spectacular from on high?

As for Isaiah, had he in mind no "worst case" alternatives, no tactics of passive resistance, just in case? Or would such hypotheses (if they do such and such, we will respond with such . . .) have been taken amiss by a jealous Yahweh?

Are we perhaps missing the point, attributing to an earlier time such speculations as stem from fairly recent understanding? For Isaiah, was the question simply one of unquestioning obedience? If, to the confusion of all mundane expectations, God seldom (or never!) shows a hand in our favor, are we then as powerless as our God? Is admitting such as this an acid test of godly conduct? In our day, does reliance on Yahweh imply that we grow venturesome, that we imagine and experiment in ways of translating the will of this nonviolent God of ours?

Of such matters we know something—and have much yet to learn.

To return to Isaiah and Hezekiah: After the huge Assyrian forces withdrew, the king became ill. He was endowed with no great store of courage, as was evident long before. Now, stricken, he turned his face to the wall and uttered a prayer that, on the face of it, seems inordinately self-justifying (showing no great store of self-knowledge either!): "'Remember, Lord, that I have served you faithfully and loyally, and that I have always tried to do your will.' And he began to cry bitterly" (Isa. 38:2–3, see also 2 Kings 20:2–3).

Once again, enter Isaiah bearing a promissory word. The sentence of death is mitigated; the king will recover. Better yet, some fifteen years of additional life are allotted him. The king then offered a prayer, over which the spirit of Isaiah, genial and elegant, seems to hover:

38:10   In the heyday of life
        I was swept alas
        to the iron gates of death.
   11   I said in tears;
        no more to behold

my God, my Beloved,
12 Yahweh, you broke
and entered
my firm-set dwelling.
13 Walls fell
as though tissue rent
in high winds flying, then
flung aside.
14　　　My life
scattered, shattered!
15 And what shall I answer,
what protest?

16 Protect me, cherish
all my plaint and prayer!

17 Draw me forth
bodily
from the pit
18 where Death and Hell
in ravenous concert
asunder
break my bones!
19 Life,
God of the living
I pray you, grant.
20 Brief,
lengthened they be—
life's days
to you given, in praise!

Hezekiah's prayer seems Isaian in its plangent tone of confidence, its dread of death and sweetness of spirit. It is as though either the king had learned something of substance from his seer (and none too soon, we would venture) or perhaps the Isaian school composed the oracle and placed it on the lips of the king.

Yet, once again the king tested the patience of Isaiah. When a delegation arrived from Babylon, Hezekiah proceeded to offer his visitors a detailed tour; first, his palace, "his silver and gold, his spices and perfumes, and all his military equipment. . . . There was nothing in his storerooms, or anywhere in his kingdom that he did not show them" (39:2–3).

What was going on? Could this be an exercise in worldliness and pride of place? Could such a vulgar spectacle be squared with the modesty, the "otherness," the "over against" character befitting a people of covenant? The king still designs to ape the nations. He will show the Babylonians that their equal, economically and militarily, exists in the world!

Isaiah, at least, was not amused. He confronted the king, demanding an explanation. Then the whiplash: All this vulgar show is doomed. You, the king, blind as a Greek protagonist, have in effect granted the Babylonians an inventory, dramatic and detailed, of their eventual loot: "A time is coming when everything in your palace, everything that your ancestors have amassed to this day, will be carried off to Babylon."

Worse, "And they will pluck your own descendants and take them off, to become eunuchs in the court of Babylon" (39:6, 7).

All these base credentials, possessions, and weaponry have created a spurious national identity. To erase and replace it, a fearful cauterant must be applied; exile will be the very branding of God. This people, recusant as they are and apt for betrayal of covenant, are mine!

Although a future ruler and future generations stand to lose everything, yet Hezekiah greeted the news with a vile relief. Someone will pay dearly, but not he. He will not live to see the outcome of his showmanship. In a notorious phrase, he will know "peace in our time."

5

Starting Over:
The Book of Consolation
(40:1–18, 21–31)

With chapters 40–55 of the book of Isaiah we arrive at a period some two hundred years later than the lifetime of Isaiah. Perhaps these chapters are rightly thought of as a magnificent extended midrash on great-great-great grandfather Isaiah.

In the oracles that follow, the people of covenant have long since been led off to exile in Babylon—fifty years of national disgrace and humiliation! We may think of chapter 40 as the book of consolation, an irreplaceable aid in the hard task of survival. The oracles were undoubtedly sung, passed hand to hand, learned by rote, written down, perhaps covertly, circulated among the enslaved like a communal lifeline, a bloodstream.

The images of early Isaiah are altered. Such images arise as befit an awful national situation; images of facing an unpalatable reality, of surpassing, refusing, surviving. The judgment of God, so harshly uttered in the years of Isaiah, yields to an abounding tenderness. Contrasting images abound: the sorrows of exile, humiliation, tyrants, slaves, mercenaries, freedom and its loss, the desert, hope deepened and hope abandoned.

There are other images as well, heartening images of springtime and renewal, of the promise—survival of the remnant—of return and restoration.

We are not for all of that, to dream up an equivalent status for ourselves. To say that we are exiles, a despised minority, would be only an exercise in illusion. Far from being in a like plight, we are all too cozily enfranchised in our culture, at home in a Babylon become our native land.

Yet exile is an image frequently invoked by Scripture to enlighten us concerning the truth of our status—anywhere, at any time. According to Scripture, we belong elsewhere and "elsewhen," aliens, wanderers, "of whom the world is not worthy" (see Heb. 11:38). Paul further exhorts, "Be not conformed to this world" (Rom. 12:2).

Nor is this status of ours before God to be reduced to mere psychological alienation. It means something quite other; we are not the followers, at once conformist and schizoid, of God and mammon. Nor are we permitted to bargain away our discipleship at the enticement of the tempter: "All this will I give you, if falling down, you will adore me" (Matt. 4:9).

Finally, we stand opposed to the world's main pursuit, death, in all its guises, forms, enticements, and images. We are opposed, in the name of life and the God of life, and the announcement of the resurrection.

40:1   Be consoled, my people
I speak heart to heart—
walk free!

2   Your slavery is abolished,
your sins expunged!

3   Prepare in the desert
the path of Yahweh,
the caravan of return.

4   Every gorge be leveled,
every mountain cast down.

5   The glory of God revealed—
your flesh shall see God!

6   A voice commanded, "Cry out!"
And I, what shall I cry?

All flesh is grass
delicate
as flowers of the field.
7   The breath of God passes over,
the grass withers,
the flowers fade,

8   but, lo,
my Spirit, my Word
abides for all ages.

The scene is not a theophany, an underscoring of transcendence of God such as opens the book of Ezekiel. We have here instead a series of announcements spoken "heart to heart," a modest approach.

"Consolation" is a word that resumes the entire chapter. The age-long exile is nearly ended; deliverance is at hand. If we have not tasted the first, the second is meaningless.

Who of us, we might ask, dwelling peaceably and quite at home in a given culture, is in need of divine consolation? In American cities, between health clubs, boutiques, spiffy apartments, second homes and spas, citizens of a certain class and color could hardly be said to languish in exile, to say the least.

Isaiah offers the usual prophetic double-edged message here; one of comfort (which is to say, strengthening) and one of reminding. The social enslavement whose ending nears did not occur in a moral blur or blank. Sin preceded the violation of covenant. The offense was especially heinous in the violations of justice and peacemaking, as we read continually in Isaiah and the other prophets of exile and return.

The extreme penalty suffered by the people is enormously distressing if we think of it as punishment. Let us say rather that the Hebrew Bible often puts into God's hands events or consequences that we would prefer to place in our own. It is something like this: when a people violates its sworn word, the sword is unsheathed. Misfortune follows in the very nature of things.

We have only to think of the fate of the nations left to their own devices and divagations. No vengeful God is required to bring a woeful outcome to criminal activity. Consequence follows crime in the nature of the moral universe. If the nations go about their business as usual, through foreign war and domestic injustice they will pull themselves down. The nations are not only destructive in the world, they are self-destructive.

One thinks in this regard of the fall of Babylon, as recounted in the book of Revelation (chapter 18). Though surrounded by restive colonies and enemy empires, Babylon requires no external disaster, whether in nature or battle, to bring about her downfall. She falls, as it were, of her own weight. The internal contradictions of affluence and misery, cruelty and luxury, bring on the catastrophe. The event is recounted by the threnody of an angel. It is not a prophecy in the usual sense; the tense is past. Given the crimes of empire, it is a fait accompli, inevitable. There is no prelude, no indication of cause. We are left to draw our own conclusions.

With regard to the exiles of Isaiah's time, the verse brings to mind the past follies of the people. Also implied are the consequences of malice and crime. When Israel apes the nations in their native infidelity, her resemblance to the same powers grows more striking. Eventually (and perhaps rapidly) Israel becomes indistinguishable from the powers of this world. Finally she is accounted no more than another among the nations—the same arms, the same instinct for violence, the same maltreatment of enemies, the same callous attitude toward the poor and defenseless at home.

In the time of Isaiah, the ruinous melding of ethos and behavior took on a special poignancy. We are to conjure up the situation— Israel, a third- or fourth-rate power, weak, shamed, its people herded off in bondage. Isaiah never hesitated to carp and denounce; Israel had aped the nations, but it lacked the violent instruments of the nations to defend itself. Hence it fell prey to the nations. It had become in effect a worldly power; then it collapsed before a superpower.

As Isaiah recounted, in his lifetime the blessing became a curse. But wondrously, that was not all. Eventually the blessing contained in the curse was revealed; the memories of suffering served to illumine the terrible years. The deliverance shed an austere light on the enslavement.

Israel had not become a superpower. It was not another Egypt or Assyria. It was the slave population of Egypt and Assyria. Therefore it was spared the fate of the nations. Israel was not abandoned by the God of compassion, did not become a killer, oppressor, or enslaver. The resemblance to the nations did not go that far.

Ancient understanding looked on the desert as a place of combat and rebirth. There the demonic spirits lurked, there in solitude, prayer, and fasting, one's vocation was wrested from a hidden God. Thus went the story of the people of Israel and of their greatest sons, John Baptist and Christ (see Matt. 3:3). The geographic details are symbols, clues as to meaning. We have, today and then, entire cultures that are spiritual deserts; the mountains to be leveled are the arrogant pride of the nations.

Between the terrible fall from grace and the eventual return a horrendous "meantime" has intervened. During that hiatus, when a rictus of imperial fury and vengeance exploded, something was learned and was absorbed into the moral energies and imagery of the tribe: We are not the nations, we are not the betrayer, enslaver, oppressor; and, above all, we are resolved once more to be keepers of our sworn word. We are, dare we say it, and despite all, chosen. But we arrogate the word with a new understanding; chosen in order that we might choose—God and one another—a people of justice, justified by the God of justice.

So the people return, chastened, poor, compassionate, totally other than the people who went forth. They went forth without God, and hopeless; they return, led by the "glory of God." The rough is made smooth, the mountains leveled, the valleys filled. The images are drawn from an ecology humanized and grown modest. A welcoming earth celebrates in all its awakening splendor, the procession of return. The images of joyous nature in communion with the pilgrims are, in the last instance, images of conversion of heart.

The transition in verse 6 is a subtle one. At the heart of these momentous events, Isaiah stands in converse with God. The message, "All flesh is as grass," communicates a sense of transience and fragility, of life at the sharp edge and the mordancy of death.

According to the Bible, there do not exist two species of humans, one immortal, the other fragile as grass. *All* flesh is grass, insists Isaiah; all human life is fragile, transitory. Grass, whether sown in imperial acres or a slave compound, is easily cut down. Even if it survives its span and prospers awhile, its season passes, and it withers or is trodden underfoot. There is no immortal grass. Grass is easily seeded, largely adaptable, fruitful, thrives in almost any soil. Then it dies, like us.

A further disturbing word comes in verse 7. The breath of God, that Spirit we name Holy, comes to us, not to bestow immortality on that flesh it has named grass, not to guarantee our prevailing, our immunity from the withering season. Quite the opposite, the Spirit of God, uttering the word of God, comes to hasten the natural process. It is like an unseasonal sirocco, hot and withering, a scorcher. It is death-bearing.

The word comes as re-minder, salvaging us from the mindless fantasy of immortality. It saves us, not from dying, but from dying badly; from dying under the fantastic notion that we will never die. It saves us from servitude to that fantasy and its consequence; a life that is a rake's progress, clearing a path for our own immortality, and in the process killing many.

Come, Holy Spirit, deliver us.

It may be cold comfort to learn that something known as the "word of God" abides (v. 8) even though we do not. This word, however, is to be understood as something other than the ape of such outlandish longings as are biblically rebuked: that we shall never die.

This is a life-giving word, a resurrecting word (not an immortal word). It surpasses death by undergoing death. This word brings to life the very dead.

This is the word (Isaiah has it by heart) that raised, as though from the dead and against all odds, the defeated and enslaved in Babylon.

This word that abides is thus to be understood as the Truth that liberates when everything else bespeaks slavery, untruth, deception, and violence. The word is by no means at peace, abiding and honored in a kind of prelapsarian paradise. No, the word is spoken against the prevailing gales, in a world of cruelty and murder—a Word therefore of conflict, tragedy, combat. In such a world the word of God barely gains a hearing. It is scarcely audible, rarely attended to in the absurd cacophony of competing claims, the culture of noise, inadvertence, and distraction.

In accord with the imagery of Isaiah, the word levels mountains (pride), fills in valleys (hebetude, routine, fatalism, numbing). Thus the word of God clears the way for a return, a journey of the spirit to self-understanding, to sanity, to nonviolence, to reverence and rejoicing, to a mystical coherence of mind and heart with creation.

We see also, alas, that the liberating word may well become an impenetrably foreign tongue, even to those who are by presumption favored of God. The crimes of the "chosen" speak louder than words, words, words—they speak of violence, self-aggrandizement, and pride. Indeed, the crimes awaken the blood of the innocent; the blood finds a voice, cries "murder!" And the word of God is a judgment.

Not every mountain has been leveled. One remains in place, firmly founded. There the herald mounts, in this instance to celebrate the coming of Yahweh:

> 40:9 Stand then, herald
> atop a high mountain—
> into four winds my word
> cry aloud—Joy!
> 10 Behold the arm of Yahweh
> invincible, ever sustaining,
> 11 as a shepherd gathers
> errant lambs to breast,
>
> bent to you, embracing you!
>
> (40:9–11)

When life comes to resemble a dog's worried bone of bare survival, when death is at the door and huffing down the chimney, when "down and out" describes both the cupboard and rooftree, then something may be thought to happen, an intervention.

The joyous messenger climbs the highest peak and shouts for all his worth, "Behold, the arm of Yahweh!"

Out of slavery God comes as liberator. How often we have heard that refrain in our lifetime! Invariably though, it comes with a rub, a raw wounding of our pride. The joyful shout of the messenger comes invariably from a foreign mountain, a mountain to the south of us . . . a peak of the Andes?

It is as though we could not bear a word of ecstasy, as though God could not conceivably come among us, among such as us, as liberator. We are all but carried under by a terrible sense (and perhaps the sense is as accurate as it is painful), a sense that God, if God there be, comes to the northern continent in a far different guise than the epiphany offered the multitudes of the south. God comes among us in judgment, not in joy.

Yet a stolen or borrowed joy is better than none. We need not go so far afield and come home so empty of hand and heart. Despite all our crimes, our empty lives, the liberator God moves us to song; "He gave joy, joy, joy into my heart." In proportion as we who dwell in the belly of the beast stand with the victims, withstand Gargantua, joy is ours also.

The message of the herald, it goes without saying, implies a scornful resistance against the conventional politics of power—sleazy as that game is, and fitfully arrogant and foolish by turn. We do not look to imperial authority for our cue. Now rejoice!

"The arm of Yahweh" (v. 10) is God's invincible strength. We take our cue quite simply and directly from the text—as well as from those believers across the world who invoke a like strength, amid the most atrocious suffering. The nations of Isaiah's time battened off the labors of a slave population. They also periodically exposed slaves and booty to the public gaze, in obscene spectacles of power.

What a strikingly different application here! The victor is revealed, not as a warrior in the service of the emperor, but as a shepherd, that least harmful and belligerent of beings. The arm of God is a tender enclosure; it enfolds the helpless and harmless. Thus strength and gentleness are united. (Ezekiel takes up the image in 34:1–6, as do Luke and John.)

When the messenger cries out (v. 9), "Behold the arm of Yahweh," we are (but only momentarily) left in the dark. "Yes," we respond; or, "It may be so, but what does God look like?"

40:12 Who among you
    measures in hand's palm
    the waters of seven seas?
    Who lays a rod

against high heaven's vault,
weighs the planet in a bowl,
mountains in a scale?

13   Does one among you whisper
        sage advice
        to Yahweh?
14   Shall he turn to you
        seeking
        just eventualities?
15   No.
        You great ones—
        droplets
        on a heated grill.
        Hold a scale aloft,
        place in the balance
        a pinch of dust—
        your sum, near nothing.
        . . . .
18   Come then,
        stand if you dare
        face to very face
        with God!

Isaiah raises the question of faith, or he treats of faith as a question, with strong overtones of Job. Who rules, who merits the name "providence"? Do the nations? They pretend so, they propagandize and present themselves as agents of boundless goodness in the world. In verses 15 to 17 an answer of sorts is offered. It is altogether indirect and yet altogether to the point.

We are urged to look abroad. Behold the world of nature, its splendid rhythms, its unity in diversity, its unfailing bounty! We may arrive, through these sublime realities, at an inkling of the mystery, the presence, the spirit that dwells within all things, the God who is provident of a creation most beloved.

Who other than the spirit of God teaches the way of God? Does there exist some mysterious entity who shall instruct God and ourselves in ways godly? The nations, forsooth?

The implied irony recalls Job. Here it is not the notorious friends of Job who are playing god, however ineptly and foolishly. It is the nations.

Yet to this day the charade continues. There exist those institutions and their sponsors who play godling, push idolatry, announce a better way than the word of God—a better way, they claim, than compassion or nonviolence or the cross.

To speak truthfully, this announced way is an improvident and irresponsible way. It involves greed, wanton killing, victimizing, foolishness, and fumbling with the integrity of creation, the incanting of death as savior.

The nations, these purportedly immortal principalities, are idolaters, pure and simple. They entice to their side the gods of iron, gods of death.

What of the God of Isaiah? They would make of this God a dependent, an appendage, a "useful option," a kind of court chaplain, if not a court jester.

This Isaiah of chapter 40 is relentless, intent on the truth. He would have us instructed as to the truth concerning the nations. The images that follow are deflating, implacable, a judgment. The nations are "droplets on a heated grill," a "pinch of dust," weightless, useless.

The nations of all ages, taken together, concentrated as to power and might, placed on the scales of God's judgment, are simply a zero. In merit and holiness they count for nothing and less than nothing. Indeed, of such realities as Isaiah speaks they know nothing.

Worse, the nations are in principle the sworn enemies of holiness. They slay the just or imprison them or "disappear" them. Thus, as chief and stark evidence of the Fall, they guarantee and underscore, while time lasts, the presence and power of death in the world.

In God's eyes, the nations are akin to a black hole in creation, a moral void.

These verses are a bitter diatribe, but Isaiah is more than the bitter oracle of an enslaved people (though he is that also). We have here a tradition, millennial, remarkably consistent, preserved and explored and insisted upon in good times and ill, by prophet after prophet. The tradition is in the blood.

Its message is this: we are not to forget, to lose our hold upon the word of God as to our vocation (which is in effect much akin to the vocation of the prophet). To forget in this sense has the most serious moral consequence. Shortly or in the long run, the amnesiac falls in line. He is seduced and enlisted as votary of this or that illusion, ideology, hoax, of whatever empire. The latest war is "just," the latest evil is the "lesser," the current candidate for the political Olympus at long last will bring "change."

In contrast, our magnificent, stubborn, ardent, and skeptical by turn, crusty sages, the prophets, offer no sellout, no obfuscation. They cast a cold eye on the blandishments and jugglery of the high and mighty. They cannot be cajoled, placated, bought off. They know not a whit of dread at being perennially in the minority—even a minority of one.

They stand in the imperial presence, not as lapdogs or sycophants or apologists, but to loose the thunders of God's judgment, denouncing the crimes of the inhuman nabobs and, often as not, paying up. They thereby offer a luminous icon of the human—as God would have us also.

Prophecy is a harsh and dreadful work. It stands between a stone and a hard place. This Isaian spirit learned his lesson in a hard school indeed, in Babylon and Egypt, exile and slavery. Is he obsessive? If so, so be it. He harps on essentials barely salvaged from the dung heap of empire.

Have we been able, in such times as literally drive many mad, to salvage something of sanity? If so, have we not found that our souls were ransomed, salvaged by the likes of Isaiah?

Whence but from these few unsubdued spirits will we come on the truth of life today, distorted, twisted, throttled as that truth is by the megamachinery of untruth?

In an election year the airwaves and video waves heat up. Promises, promises pollute the air; glib henchmen utter their foolishness, the media echo like a cave of bats—mewings, strokings, choler, anger, vituperation, verbal abuse and scufflings, much dust flung about, no clarity. Bread and circuses are expended broadside, money seduces and unsettles and buys and sells opinions and promises that are of absolutely no sense or worth.

40:21 Dwellers upon earth,
be mindful, be attentive
to Alpha-Omega!

. . . .

23 Princes high and mighty—
a breath, I bring you down.
24 Judges overweening
I unseat you, strip you
naked to the winds.

25 Who dares then
seize the initiative?
26 Raise your eyes
to the firmament—
under that majesty
learn true measure!

(40:21–26)

The questioning resumes. Can you not comprehend at last, the most primitive truths? Has idolatry so infected as to blind you to your own tradition?

They (we) no longer literally know who we are. Rapidly or slowly, but in any case surely, we have grown deaf to the music of the spheres, as they hymn the praise of the Creator.

We hop about the land like witless grasshoppers, Isaiah says. We are here, there, and, at first frost, gone.

The image extends also to the so-called great ones. If the people are thoughtless revenants, come and vanished in a season, what of the princes and judges, kings and rulers? They are of even less moment than their subjects; they are stuck, reduced to the vegetative world, one with the grasses of the field (v. 24). Scarcely are they planted in place, shallowly rooted, when the rude winds of time blow them away.

A scornful challenge is flung at them in verses 25 and 26: Look about at the pantheon of godlings cluttering the earth. It is as though Mount Olympus and its bickering, uneasy coven had invaded planet earth. All manner of idols pollute ground and air and sea. In the shrines money and appetite and ego and hatred are celebrated; death is invoked and venerated. Who indeed undertakes this dangerous work of creating the gods?

The grasshopping humans are apt symbols of a human sense that has been shrugged off in pursuit of other goods. The votaries seek power, and in the dark quest they lose all sense of scope and limit.

The images evoke a multitude, leaders and led alike. They are plowed into the natural processes and rhythms of time. They are lost there.

The faithful are offered a better way. "Raise your eyes to the firmament." Take note of the stars. They are hardly nameless, anonymous, any more than the sparrow who falls (see Luke 12:6). The names of stars or sparrows, like our own, are conferred by God and dearly cherished. They are thus a mirror and reminder of vocation—God's and our own. God enters the human order, names things.

Stewardship, responsibility; these are godlike activities, and in that measure human. Stewardship toward the very stars? Yes. Raise your eyes to them; let your awe be their honor. Your vocation embraces all creation, from the grandest being to the humblest, outspread under the noble vault of heaven.

40:27   Why this plaint, my people?
        is your God forsooth
        indifferent, unmoved,
        no tears upon your trouble,
        no heart to mourn your heart's
        losses and lesions?
28   Only see!
        endearing, forebearing,
        I uphold the world,
        enduring, upbearing!
29   and you—
        I keep your tears
        close and accounted,
        your name
        writ in my hand's palm
        least, last though you be—

no, not lost.
The fallen sparrow
I breathe to life,
an epiphany:

30   "Little one, arise,
drink the rainbow,
sing a new song, schooled
by larks and nightingales!"
No envy then, no dark looks.
Youth, age, join hands!
An elder are you?
trust, hope in Yahweh—
31   be renewed, dream eagles,
on high
mount, drink the sun!

(40:27–31)

It is God's turn to question the questioners. These, be it noted, are by no means the faithless. They have raised their eyes to the firmament, to the stars. Those who come questioning the light are no whit less faithful for that. Now God questions them, a neat turnabout, albeit a painful one.

The matters raised are hardly to be thought frivolous. The faithful have endured terrible times; they are exiles, ex-slaves, who emerge from generations of suffering—from insuperable fidelity. Burdened with such memories, wounded survivors as they are, how could their faith take other form than a questioning of God? How long, O Lord? How much longer?

Is relief underway? Is the promise soon to be honored?

Their situation is precarious. A taste of freedom is in the air, but it must not be confounded with freedom itself. Rumors, possibilities fly and flounder about. For captives, any captives, the deepest doubts arise just before dawn, at the threshold of desire.

No breakthrough is evident as yet. The meager light of predawn seems spurious, a mirage—even as it is infinitely desirable. At such a time, the earth grown cold, the dawn coming ever so slowly, the longing is deepest, and the sense of possible betrayal is most vivid.

At this crucial point, even the most faithful spirits grow faint.

Still, creation itself offers reassurance. The covenant is written in uncial and minuscule, from the stars to the grasses of the field:

Let us speak of your weariness, your doubts. I say in response, I do not grow weary, I do not doubt you.

Remember my knowledge (which appears to you an enigma), my being from eternity (which in your fragile temporal sojourn, you so fear).

I bring up such matters, such truths, not to traumatize. Quite the opposite. My knowledge and my eternal being are in service to you. Foreknowledge, eternity itself, are for your sake, a promise, a gift and compassionate overflow.

I am the absolute, for the sake of you, relative as you are, and vulnerable, put upon, fragile, like grass of the field.

I am the eternal who sanctions, not your death, but your resurrection. My existence guarantees your own, as a mother's her unborn. My existence holds in providential hands your doubt-ridden, perplexed, calamitous life.

Your hope, you say, is in the young? Alas, your young women and men are grass also. They give up, give in. Their spirits droop; they fall away. They join the ranks either of the vegetating powerful or the witless grasshoppers, those who prosper for a season, then fall to naught.

But in whom are you to rely, you ask, if not in the young? You raise the wrong hope, this cult of youth. Therefore hope falls short. For this affair called hope is not a virtue of the young nor of the aged either.

It is my hope for you and of yours for me and of yours for one another. All ages, all conditions!

Look, a transfusion of hope in every human vein, youthful or aged. I name you, therefore, those who "hope in Yahweh." And I promise—youths, elders—you will be no more earthbound than eagles are.

6

Servanthood and Betrayal: The Human Spectrum

Four passages within chapters 42 through 53 of the book of Isaiah have received particular attention through the years. Collectively, they are known as the "servant songs." What a joy to recall that God's word is often a poetic one, a celebration, not a cerebration. These passages are meant to be recited or sung! Each describes certain aspects of one known as the servant of Yahweh. Although there has been much speculation about the identity of this servant in history, no one has been able to name a particular person who fills this role. We have no inkling as to the servant's identity, whether she or he is intended as more than a type. She might be someone, anyone, who suffers and dies for sake of the truth, one of the anonymous heroes who perishes and is shoveled into an unmarked grave.

Comes Now My Servant, Gentle and Faithful
(42:1–4, 5–8)
The First Song of the Servant of Yahweh

42:1   Comes now my servant;
look how I upbear her,
this chosen one
in whom my soul delights!

My spirit outpoured,
my justice her own!

2 Her mind no proving ground
whence vexing thoughts bestir,
how gently she walks the earth!
small creatures safe and sound,
unharmed, close cherished.

3 Her soul
borne on high
an unextinguished flame
routing the dark.

4 Faithful, unconquerable—
the ends of the earth hearken,
lauding that Word of truth—
her, my own!

This passage, a celebrated oracle of Isaiah, is indeed one of the most beloved passages of all Scripture. Who of us does not long to believe that we are called, named, chosen, sent? Meaning, identity, and other such catchwords as are current in psychology, start here. Still, to the servant of God, such ways of arriving at self-knowledge would seem utterly banal. One does not open the Scripture for the kind of self-scrutiny promised (and often vainly promised) by psychiatry. We find something other, something of God's will for us and a measure of insight into ourselves.

We are in the presence of God and, at the same time, of the human. The essence of the human is clarified—the one who is called, chosen, elected. The servant belongs to God, is one with God. Thus the servant is presented to us; better, she is celebrated, and we are invited in. She does not present or celebrate herself. Light falls on the Other in whose shadow (or light) the servant stands, dances, and rejoices.

A dynamism is at work, a task underway. The cords of Adam (and Eve) are tightly drawn; they are in the hands of the transcendent One. Grace is the drawing of those cords ever closer, urging the beloved closer to the Other.

For not only is the servant chosen; "in whom [her] my soul delights"(NRSV); "whom my soul prefers" (JB). Ecstasy, the delight of God is in the air, awakened by the presence, the life of the servant.

This choice of God is a delicate matter. Are others not also loved and singled out? One must believe so, lest matters of religion, race, or color take on a questionable form. In classical Jewish commentary, the Servant Song was understood as a celebration of God's choice of a community. The loving and summoning voice extended out and out. If Jews were chosen, it was in order to offer a sign of loving compassion in the world. The everlasting arms enfolded all. Let us then refuse to read the text from the point of view of ego, whether personal or political. Simply in being chosen, one becomes a sign of God's choice of everyone. Indeed our creation, our existence, and the joy of walking the world indicate a primal choice of humans on the part of God. From the start we are blessed, summoned, and rejoiced in.

Baptism and confirmation are occasions to accept once more that first choice, to choose to be chosen. Symbolically we follow through on the first act of God, echo the divine yes with our own. Thus we find our dignity and our vocation.

Therefore we take joy in all the living, the unborn, the rejected and despised, those declared expendable, the aged (so often also unwanted). We welcome them all! We rejoice in each and every one!

"My spirit outpoured, my justice her own!" This godly spirit immediately appoints a task, a vocation. When God's spirit rests upon the servant, questions of justice immediately arise, like ghosts at a banquet. The mandate is quite simple: Go, make justice among the nations.

Deprived of or actively despising the Spirit of God, the nations are deprived also of justice, its capacity or practice, indeed its very notion. Left to its own devices and resources, conventional secular power is capable only of injustice, a void at the heart. This unjust behavior has no warrant; it is a hellish summons, demonic. It is denied all validity by the word of God.

The nations, wherever named in Isaiah, are by biblical definition unjust. They traffic in injustice; they glory in it; they demand unconditional surrender to a system that stands outside the law, self-legitimating. They wage horrid wars for gain by the supreme injustice of murder, lands, markets, and colonies for despoiling.

Thus they crown themselves and raise the scepter of hegemony over time and this world.

This very old story is often repeated and just as often forgotten in the telling. The imperial nations succeed one another, mime one another, learn nothing, repeat ad nauseam the old bloody rigmarole.

Will the unjust one day be reborn, become just? Such will certainly occur, but only by a miraculous outpouring of the spirit. Then the world, the nations and their systems, will be no more. The realm of God will be upon us.

Thus justice, often seen as an admirable possession of the nations, is by no means to be understood as the fruit of natural evolution, or of this or that form of revolution. Considering the history of secular power, so unlikely is the advent of this virtue that justice must be called quite simply an act of God.

Still, the text does not concentrate so much on the conversion of the nations as on the vocation of the servant. The servant is the savior of the nations, quite literally. The servant is a lonely forerunner, a first presence and sign of an act of God. The life of the servant is a blessing in the midst of a curse.

In patience and steadfastness and courageous speech, the servant is a witness that the plight of the unjust, awful as it is and seemingly beyond redemption, is not entirely hopeless.

Let the servant be born and summoned. Let her stand there, speak the truth, face the murderous plaint, "How long O Lord, how long?"

The servant does not know.

Our text is seemly and reticent on the vexed subject of how and when the justice of God is to prevail. As we are reminded in another place, "But about that day and hour no one knows, neither the angels of heaven" (Matt. 24:36 NRSV). Our text is no magical key opening the future; it is rather like a holy manual of instruction.

Announce justice to the nations, live in hope, grow not weary. And meantime, bear with that event to come, that "not yet." Do not attempt to seize the times, as though the future were in your hands, or the past, or for that matter, the present. Rather, hold on to something other, something as precious as it is rare. Do so that despite all, in face of opposition and terror, there may exist a trace, a hint, a foreshadowing of that most unlikely, defamed, dreaded reality—justice, the justice of God.

Simultaneously (and justly), seek the abolition of the sword, an end to war. Put an end to playing God on the part of would-be godlings, idolatry, the prevailing crime of systems that claim life and death power over the living. Let there be no more smart bombs and smart bombers on the prowl, on the ready, on the hair trigger. Let there be no more nukes, no more weapons research and huckstering, no more savage experimenting on the flesh and bone of innocents.

Let there be, simply, no more injustice, no more justice systems mocking true justice, delaying the realm of justice, masking the injustice, fossilized, totalized, embedded as it is in the marrow of creation. The end of warmaking would signal at once the spirit of God dwelling in the nations and the coming of God's realm. Isaiah has said so (2:4), "swords into plowshares."

Yet the justice of God is hardly to be thought native to the nations. It is something other—an import, gift, unknown quantity. Justice does not flourish in any climate or soil of this world. Of this we are assured.

And yet . . . and yet, it remains incontestible that justice is the vocation of the nations, in spite of all, in spite of themselves. They know nothing of it and care less. Should it appear in the person of the servant, in whatever political form or attempted form, the just one must be violated, prosecuted, denied, put to scorn, scotched, botched, cut down.

The servant is a lonely spirit, most often dwelling in desert places or prisons, far from the centers of power and recognition. The servant embodies a spirit often defamed, derided, dealt with in utmost harshness, as it was in the case of Isaiah and later, in the imperial justice system that seized on servant Jesus.

The realism of Isaiah is striking. He probes the spiritual physiognomy of the servant. Can the servant stand, and withstand? For in face of the demand that justice be done, opposition arises like a tidal wave. Resistance comes not only on the part of the nations, but also from the church in its frequent complicity with injustice, celebrating the presumed sanctity or righteousness of the nation.

Sanctity, righteousness, and all are spurious. "Under God," as they say. Under God, and unjust.

In verses 2–4, we are offered a moral image of the servant—gentle, strong, steadfast. We gain some light on the text by pondering the conduct of the servant Jesus. Indeed, Matthew applies this passage to Jesus (12:17–21). We note in Jesus a confident self-awareness, a calm reliance on the prevailing power of the truth, a sense of modesty and human scope. Yet Jesus did not invariably sail through tranquil waters; quite the contrary. The Gospels also recount much palaver and debate in the streets and elsewhere, one-to-one and with large crowds. Jesus did not suffer hostile and hypocritical adversaries with an unvarying calm mein. Quite the contrary, we are offered extraordinarily scathing diatribes, denunciations, judgments, manifestos, even ultimatums.

There are ways and ways of raising one's voice, of getting heard in the streets. There are the ways of the world. They are like the babblings of ventriloquist dolls, wired to the culture, the volume tuned up and up, devouring, deafening. Such voices long to be found "relevant," but intemperance condemns them to utmost irrelevance. They mime love of ego, money, power, violence. Thus does the medium succeed in scrambling the message, especially the "religious" message.

There are the other ways, transparent, hopeful, nonviolent, the many moods and tones, rhythms, joys, and furies of the Spirit who is said to dwell in the servant. Medium and message are one, fused in that fire. The voice of the servant is raised, is indeed heard, loud and clear and in public.

But the outcry is preceded by a long apprenticeship in listening—a time often passed in desert places, catching the message of the winds and sun and stars, taking the truth to heart, wrestling for its possession against the inhabiting demons. Finally the servant is possessed by the word, becomes its finely tuned instrument.

Likewise, we need not prove anything; we need not justify ourselves. Indeed, we are sternly reminded of the One who alone justifies. We need only heed our calling to speak the truth, in season and out, trusting to the power of the truth to win a hearing, whether ears be keen or deaf.

The servant of God treats tenderly the fragile beauties of creation, for she sees in them an image of her own soul. Therefore, neither quenching nor breaking, she is neither quenched nor broken.

One moves gently about the earth and so learns strength. In treating with needful care things easily destroyed, one goes from strength to strength. There are other ways, of course. There are the theory and practice of domination, the mastery and control of institutions, persons, and creation itself. In such an instance, someone must pay, and pay dearly. Lives are broken and quenched, misery abounds.

Towers, secular and sacred pretensions, thrusting upward on the urban landscape, here and there and everywhere, assert that possession and power are impregnable, nine points of the law. The towers are there, and all they stand for, all they proclaim, all they deny and ignore—the luxury that creates and maintains the misery, the poor and homeless who are mortised into those mighty foundations and perish there, bones, bones, dry bones.

We in the church, breaking the reed, quenching the flame as we do, are ourselves broken and quenched. We misuse the earth and its resources, defraud the poor, while setting up a kingdom of manipulation and security. The buzz and palaver, the workshops and committees, the five- and ten-year plans, the evangelization schemes, the hubbub around communications, all these proliferate under the aegis of canny churchmen [sic]. Such interminable wearying efforts put to an end, once for all, such unpleasant matters as insecurity, improvisation, life at the side of the poor, and hearkening to the Spirit. In consequence, little is said and less done about bringing justice to earth.

The text is so clear. Out of injustice, systemic, abstract, straight-faced, out of such systems, whether decked out in secular or churchly robes, justice cannot rise or be proclaimed.

We conduct ourselves as though the end justified shady and despicable means. We are consequently in great need of a Gandhi or Isaiah to assure us otherwise, and sternly. Indeed, truthful instructors are agreed that the means are one with the end. And the end, if it is to remain recognizably good, demands that the means be scrutinized, corrected, reproved, and variously abandoned or strengthened.

How does one become teachable, attentive to simple and lowly things—candle flame endangered in the winds, reeds more fragile than the bones of small birds? The vulnerability and mortality of the symbols urge us to pause and to grow mindful. The flame, the reed, are more than simple phenomena, to be passed by, more or less contemptuously or thoughtlessly trodden upon.

All things are to be cherished and protected, as a hand cupped over a flame, or a gentle footfall upon the earth. We too are fragile. Someone must not quench us or crush us.

We name this mindful One, Providence.

In so describing the Servant, God describes herself. The qualities praised in the Servant are literally godly, as the life and death of Jesus illustrate.

42:5   In the beginning
       (I the beginning)
       all things left my hand.
       You, clay gently kneaded.
       Lover, mouth to mouth,
       I breathed,
       you breathed, newborn.
    6   Now hand in hand
       we walk the world.
       You, as though clean parchment—
       my covenant, your flesh
       writ. You, the living text.
    7   My work, my wonders, yours;
       to open blind eyes
       to lead forth the captives!

       . . . .
    8   These, yes
       ever greater works, await!

The credential is creation, here as elsewhere in our Bible (v. 5). It is the Creator of the world who speaks, the One who gives breath and spirit to humans.

The images are all of life, the vitality, variety, and verve of the world, the spirit that animates all. The God of life summons us to life. More, God summons us to be life-givers, especially toward those who lie under the heel of the powers. The work of justice is the moral crown of the work of creation itself, the completion of the creative task of Genesis.

"Clay gently kneaded . . . mouth to mouth I breathed."

I have formed you (as in Gen. 2:7) as a covenant to the people and light of the nations. The human vocation stretches far and wide, a passionate outreach. God's servant people are the hand of the arm of God.

We know the character of that vocation to justice today mainly through its heroes, peacemakers, servants. We also know the vocation through its opposite as our horrified gaze rests on the injustice that proliferates across the world, a pandemic darkness.

The crimes of the nations! Social, financial, political, and military collusion creates multitudes of victims. Injustice is built into entire systems; a summons to even minimal justice is rarely heard and even more rarely acted upon. Numbing of spirit afflicts the mighty, a kind of numbed despair the citizenry. If here and there the poor raise an outcry, a gag—worse—is promptly applied.

We note pridefully the penalties being exacted of Christians today in our land and elsewhere. Pridefully, painfully, we give thanks, knowing beyond doubt that the kangaroo courts, jailings, torture, disappearances, and deaths befit a scriptural people.

Verse 7 is particularly poignant, hinting at our history, our long connivance with the powers of darkness. Yet, in spite of it all, we have been healed of our blindness and led out of the past, a prison indeed. We have attained the light. We think of the base communities, the liberation theologies, the suffering servants of the third world—and the first.

Once healing has occurred, the newly healed emerge; they are now healers. The public work, the proffer of relief and reconciliation is underway. The servant, or better, the community of servants, takes the people to heart. In a community of servants, justice is proclaimed.

The covenant is honored, a light struck. Women are respected, children are cherished. Money is not enthroned, nor ego nor pride of place. Such attentiveness to modest essentials is a setback to the principalities; it is the start of great things in the world.

We have a slight sense of this momentous occurrence today. The Latin peasants awaken to the theft of honor, land, dignity, work, money, education, health, housing, everything, at the hands of the oligarchs. The truth of life, the honor accruing to life, all that gives life its aura, meaning, hope, and future, are snatched away. To talk of a different social or economic order is no more than a pipe dream. Yet, ever so slowly, against all odds, a biblical sense of outrage arises, of forced dislocation, of being robbed of one's very humanity by a usurping power.

The primordial claim is stated, shouted in anger. I know my own name! You may not rob me of it! My name, which is to say, power, vocation, uniqueness, honor. My soul is my own; no one owns me. No one can claim my rightful place, my sanctuary, my land, my future, my world.

We have heard such rage before, uttered by the prophet in the name of God. It is God who has summoned the Servant (v. 6) to serve the covenant of justice, not the idols. The idols, it goes without saying, cannot serve the one who serves justice; they can only confuse, misserve, and set human matters awry.

The passion of the Servant echoes the cry of God; that God's honor and glory be given to no other (42:8).

It cannot be said too often that the works of justice, the vocation of the Servant, are the preeminent form of honoring and glorifying God. They are true worship.

Yahweh, Must I Expend All for Small Return or None? (49:1–6)

The Second Song of the Servant of Yahweh

49:1 People, give ear!
from the womb of my mother
Yahweh summoned me,
from her breast Yahweh spoke my name.

2 My words
sharp as a sword;
hid in his quiver
me, a ready arrow.

3 Appointed me: "You, servant
in whom my honor abides."

4   Still, a double mind
    casts me about:
    "How I expend, Sir,
    and all in vain, life
    upon Thy cause!"

    And yet … and yet—
    I know,
    beyond doubt's craven shadow
    my strength, my honor lies
    in Yahweh, no other
    whose loving reproof—
    "Is it then matter
    of small weight or none,
    that my anointing
    like balm in Gilead
    strengthen you,
    far though you venture
    or near abide?"

We are here offered a song of vocation and consequence. It is also a song of contrasting, even contrary rhythms—power and weakness, strength and failure of nerve. Through it, a sublime calling makes itself heard, like a great gong sounding in the heart of the servant, a bell note signifying death or rebirth, or perhaps both. The servant hears and rejoices, yet at the same time feels an all but overpowering sense of inadequacy. What is one to do, where is one to go, with such a weighty summons? Will strength be granted to respond, to be faithful?

The servant shouts urgently into the winds (v. 1), even into adverse winds. Let those afar take heed, as well as those near at hand! The claim of the servant, the vivid, urgent sense of self, of direction and vocation, is of some consequence, not only for the calling of the servant but also because the story of the servant of God is the story of all. In every life, at its very inception, God has intervened. All are to embody the word of God.

Before my birth, before my parents thought to name me, God pronounced my name. The name stands for a primordial choice, vocation, summoning. It beckons one out of the anonymous and disregarded, sets one aside, exempt from the world's savage terms of worth—production, money, and ego.

God's naming sets the terms of existence and signifies both travail and hope for all one's lifetime, until death and beyond. Before one could pronounce one's name, someone had announced it. Before self-knowledge, there was the knowledge of Another—who this unknown one would be, where this life would venture. Before one could set foot to an errand in the world, or so much as gain an inkling of one's direction, both errand and direction were sure.

Here we touch a question of humanism: What is a human being?

The unborn one is—in the eyes of Another—someone. Someone penetrates the darkness of prebirth. In that darkness, in one's own mind, one cannot as yet be anyone at all. Yet into that darkness, on that unconscious helpless being, the glance of God comes to rest. She holds the unborn in her love, close as a mother's womb.

How many ways, one reflects, there are to abort this insight, to hold life cheap, one's own or the lives of others. Killing abstractions dispose of others, strip the name conferred by God, abandon people to sword or famine, to war, or some such meaningless term as "overpopulation."

We stand in the midst of this moral shambles and mourn. We are the witnesses of a massive misnaming, denaming of those named by God. This is the demonic course of empire in our lifetime, as in that of Isaiah. He too mourned the plight of the powerless and poor, the exiles, those under siege. So he must all the more vehemently vindicate the love that does not abandon or grow weary.

Thus Isaiah launches diatribes against idolatry. Those who misname humans misname God. They give over the glory of God to sticks and stones. For Isaiah idolatry was not merely a religious question devoid of human, political consequence. The disenfranchising of humans, by way of slavery, murder, stigma, devaluing, despising, ostracism, does not stop there. The business of empires is also the (strictly understood) business of idolatry. Maltreatment of humans, denying them a name, naming them for death, cheapening and devaluing the living, is a summons to the idols: Come, make the world your killing field.

The gods of death seize upon the structures of empire, make of them what we call a no-man's-land. There, in defiance of the God of life, they multiply images of death. The ever more sophisticated arsenals of weaponry are researched, bought and huckstered, and inevitably put to use across the world.

Further, if God has conferred on humans the dignity of a name, it is in order that we may name things, name creation. This implies, among other things, judgment. We are called, in the inelegant phrase, to "call the shots." Yet we note another power, a far different one, at work in our world. The idols confer on their votaries the awesome, deranging power of misnaming creation. This goes far beyond a game of words. It means that minds and hearts are damaged in their native function—to grasp the truth, to embrace moral goodness.

Judgment and behavior are thus twisted. Crime becomes a tool of authority, murder a legitimate defense, terror a normal climate, greed and appetite a rule of thumb. The culture, at its worst and most persuasive and clamorous, calls the moral shots. What is right is whatever appears enhancing or useful or attractive to appetite, greed, ego, power—and the devil take the hindmost.

Nonetheless, the de-creators are not finally in charge, despite all pretensions. Here is our power: the word of God is taken into account. Here are the servants of Yahweh, servants of justice and truth, not of the idols, the *anawim,* the little people, those named of God, those truthfully naming creation.

While verse 2 embodies weapons imagery, the images express nonviolent realities; the sword is the power of truth, the ready arrow the right direction of mind. Neither sword nor arrow is engaged in killing. Nor is the servant so engaged.

The servant has embraced what one can only call a certain willed ignorance. She simply does not know, more, does not care, is unconcerned with such matters as outcome, result, effectiveness, and success. Concentrating on such can only mean that the substance of activity is squandered away in favor of justifying oneself, proving something. Thus we become distracted from the main issue: vocation, task, worthwhile undertaking, the hope of God.

Such willed ignorance is crucial; it might be equated with detachment of heart. It clears the terrain of the soul. One is then free to concentrate on essentials, on the goodness and truth of the task itself.

But if one makes of results or achievement one's credential, a kind of violence insinuates itself into the metaphors of Isaiah. Sword and arrow are sword and arrow, inert, ready for their one task, weapons indeed, enticing instruments of single-minded violence. They lose their power of leading beyond themselves into realms of nonviolence, lose their power of evoking mystery.

Rather than being burdened with an obsession with results, the many tasks of truth telling and truthful action carry their own credential. It is said in effect, "I the servant, the sword of Yahweh, am hidden in the shadow of God's hand. And I the arrow of Yahweh, am hidden in God's quiver."

This is a word of providence, certainly, but often providence is a mystery, a darkness. By no means does God exempt the servant from tragedy and death. The shadow is heaviest and darkest as the initial calling goes on into life. The question arises and often takes agonizing form: Shall my life go somewhere, mean something to others, mean something to God?

The arrow of our image perhaps dreams of flight, dreams of a direct hit, but all the while it is hidden in God's quiver. The arrow might never fly. Indeed of itself the arrow can go nowhere, short of the drawn bow and the hand and eye of the archer.

Who is to judge, who will deny or affirm? Different estimates are in the air; diverse opinions fly about regarding the life and work of the servant (vv. 3 and 4). The mood darkens. The servant grows disheartened; she is not at all reassured by the comfort of Yahweh.

God begins with praise of the servant: You glorify me; in you is to be found my honor. Such simple words of love, respect, admiration, such an encomium one might think ought to put to rest once and for all any reservations, second thoughts, and discouragement.

By no means! The friend of God is hardly raised to a serene ecstatic plane where worldly cares and defeats, slings and arrows, matter not a whit. The blessing of God is no such transfusion of sweetness and light.

The servant hears the word of approval and blessing. She undoubtedly is grateful—"in principle," as is often said. Yet there is the world—and the task appointed, hard and often thankless as it is. There is a work to be done; the outcome more often than not is defeat and scorn. Who has not seen the world as an obdurate wall, set firm against all consolation?

Although divine approval may be granted, the rub remains. Somewhere at the edge of conscience, never entirely quelled or put to silence, a voice speaks: "Ought not great results follow valiant efforts, the world's fury yield before patient goodness?"

The servant of God, we are told, knows utter discouragement and is worn down and beset. "All for nothing, all in vain" wells up, the heart's cry. And strange to say, we sense that we are in goodly company. The word of God is no stranger to our most terrible hour.

Effect, we are told, ought to follow cause, all else being equal. Ax laid to the root will be followed by extirpation of said root. When one's best effort is put forth, evil will be done with once for all—or at least, this evil, this once! Can the laws of logic be applied to spiritual activity, activity in favor or defense or cherishing of life?

Christ offers another way. In him, the imagination of God abides. He composes and sings servant songs of analogy and parable. Thus, by way of example, the "realm of God," that primary image of history come to term, is portrayed almost gingerly, in hidden, gradual, modest terms.

Many today point to the uneasiness awakened by the traditional term "kingdom of God." It is too close to control, patriarchy, overweening authority. The Scholars' Bible proposal of "God's imperial rule" is surely no improvement. Scandinavians recall an old Norse term meaning "the coming of the light." For Filipino Christians, the translation goes "return to one's own country." Closer to home, we have Martin Luther King's "beloved community." The Jonah House resisters and others speak simply of "kin-dom." This approximation suggests the blessing and promise, "I am with you."

Let us extend, explore the meaning, content, of the image! Conceive of the realm in new ways! A world of images is offered by Christ—better, dramatized by him—images of waiting, listening, observing, debating, healing, conveying hope and humor, telling stories that end with a question lodged like a seed in the heart.

However we translate the promise, it is by no means offered as a universal solvent, healing all wounds, comforting all distress. How could it be, in Isaiah's time or ours? Our contrary experience stands, rises on itself, a very tidal wave of tears and contradiction.

What then are we to make of repeated biblical claims that God is in charge of things? The claims must be separated from any divine policy, whether of political salvation, of stopping evil in its tracks, of blind succoring, last-minute plucking by the hair, agenda dictated from on high, wicked matters set right by command or curse, punishment or reward issued on the moment, backsliders cajoled, the infallibly right (or wrong) way pointed out, the just justified, the (presumably) wicked chastised.

We note the plaint of the servant, seeing that for all her efforts nothing of the immovable world moves. We recall also a more tragic plaint, uttered on the cross by the Servant of servants: "Why have you abandoned me?"

We too come bruisingly up against a blank wall, a veritable wailing wall, a nondialogue, the nearly unbearable tension between God's long view and the servant's anguish. Is it indeed a long view or a cul-de-sac, obscure presence or blank illusion? In any case, the terrible silence of God falls like an iron portcullis on all attempts at knowing, seeing, being consoled, assured—let alone vindicated.

And the world, that mad machine, rolls on.

Perhaps the verses in question (3 and 4) are not meant as a dialogue; perhaps they are a summing up. Each insists on the truth of a perspective; one speaking from the end of things, the other from within the travail and fury of life. Each must hear the other out. It is as though we were offered here, in two short verses, a kind of mini book of Job—faith as drama, dialogue, opposition, hope.

Verses 5 and 6 are personal, yet they sound a universal note as well. The light, once struck, enlightens all. The servant is called by name, then sent forth for the sake of others.

Is there irony in the probe, "Is it then matter of small weight or none?" urging the servant to summon a better, more cheerful mood? Is it something like, "Could you, setting out on so difficult a road, have expected not to encounter the worst of the world's wiles and contempt (as well as the worst of yourself!) along the way?

"What indeed did you expect? Because the errand was a noble one, sanctioned by God, all should go smoothly? Alas, the 'world, the way it goes' decrees otherwise.

"And did you expect to escape an interior Gorgon, so to speak—moods, downfall of hope, glooms overtaking, nothing accomplished, no meaning, Why did I ever dream of entering on such folly?"

When the servant can do very little, she can still do something. With nowhere to go, no one to turn to, tasting the lees of helplessness, still she calls out in the night.

The nearest description of her condition is a rehearsal of death. Yet it may dawn on her that she is not alone at all. She is surrounded by a multitude of others; like her they are bewildered, all but lost. They form a chorus of grief. "The Lord has forsaken me, my Lord has forgotten me."

And they win a hearing. Despite all.

Yahweh, Hasten to My Side! (50:4–9)

The Third Song of the Servant of Yahweh

50:4 Yahweh confers on me
　　　a tongue skilled and compassionate.
　5　Yahweh opened my ears;
　　　each morning I waken
　　　eager for her teaching.
　6　No quailing, not once
　　　before outrage and insult—
　　　shoulders bloodied
　　　under the lash,
　　　countenance
　　　sullied with spittle.

　　　Still, forbearance is mine;
　7　Yahweh hastens to my side,
　　　my will adamant,
　　　my soul never confounded.

　8　Lo, the Advocate nears,
　　　who then brings charges?

> let the envious take warning—
> a greater than they defends me.
> 9   My accusers?
>   they flee
> put to shame, to silence!

The servant is teachable, spiritually apt for her vocation. She, a listener, is attentive to the voice of Another. So she becomes a vessel of truth and salvation for others. Then pain enters the scene, and persecution and setback (a theme to be explored in detail in the fourth song). There can be no smooth sailing for the servant of truth. To worldly powers the message is troublesome, and worse.

The servant speaks. Her words roil the apparently calm waters. The waters in fact stink with pollution, and someone named Isaiah has a keen nose to detect it. Trouble is in the offing.

The unacceptable character of God's word inevitably revolves around matters of justice. On this point the conscience of generations untold has been formed, largely with the help of the prophets. And the contrary is true. When justice is neglected in favor of other (biblically speaking, sinful) matters, consciences have been deformed, time out of mind.

The deformation continues, indeed flourishes, in our day. Things as they are, which is to say politics as they are, war, preparation for war, maltreatment of the innocent—these have hardened into a dogma incised on tablets of stone. Rather than carrying out a closely scrutinized, accountable stewardship, subject to rebuke and even recall, authorities function (malfunction) out of all control.

Yet look closely. Fidelity, the passion for biblical justice, continues to speak up and to pay up. Herein lies our hope for just behavior, just structures.

Yet how remarkable it is that in the view of many, there is no such troublesome matter in Scripture as judgment laid against wrongful authority. The word of God is itself judged as purely apolitical. The god thus presented is of course acceptable—to the unjust above all. For such a god offers no objection, no contrary word, no rage in face of manifest injustice.

For a horrid example, recall that in November 1989 the elite military officers in San Salvador resolved on the murder of the Jesuits. Their meeting ended with a prayer to the effect that God might bless their deed. It was after all, entered on "for God and country."

God's servant touches the nerve of injustice. The cover is blown. The suppurating crime, bleeding away behind the god-talk, the god-worship, the god-prayer, the blessing from the corrupt sanctuary, the crime is revealed. Then trouble descends!

Verse 4 offers an image of a clear channel, the ear in which the word of God sounds, all unimpeded. It comes into the soul, then flows outward, from tongue and lips, to the world. The servant testifies, the word is not my own, yet it has become my own for the sake of those who are wordless—for the sake of those defeated and deafened by the ambiguous word of the world.

What a refreshment is the word of truth!

How immediate, and devastating, is the consequence! The word is no sooner spoken than hatred and persecution mount. The passage is nothing if not realistic, as though the word of God were revealing the fate of the word of God. That fate is a simple one—rejection, heedlessness, scorn. And more, the word here spoken concerns also the fate of the servant of the word, whose crime consists in this; she stands by her word.

Why then speak the word? If this is the fate of the word of God, why utter such a word?

For answer, recall the word of Jesus: "The word is the seed" (Mark 4:14). We are immediately in the realm of parables, images that speak of the likelihood and unlikelihood of the word gaining a hearing.

This parable is about parables, about where and in whom and when the word of God literally "lands." After that, the parable speaks of its fate—what interferes, inhibits, seizes, wastes, what goes wrong. Finally, the parable asks what is "good soil" (without ever defining or describing the qualities that make for goodness) and increase.

The story of the seed is told so the outsiders may look and look and not see; that they may listen and not understand. Here is what happens. With some, "as soon as they hear the message, Satan comes and takes it away." Others "receive it gladly, but it does not sink deep into them, and they don't last long." Still others "hear the message, but . . . the love for riches and all other kinds of desires crowd in and choke the message, and they don't bear fruit."

Still, the outcome is by no means entirely bleak—quite the opposite. The final message is one of hope: "Other people are like seeds sown in good soil. They hear the message, accept it, and bear fruit; some thirty, some sixty, and some one hundred."

Thus the awful report of Isaiah is modified. Not everyone turns away from the truth; there is the perennial fidelity of the few to rejoice the heart. After all, someone thought highly enough of the original bleak words of Isaiah to set them down. Someone heard—and more than one. Likewise with the story of the seed: the church received the story as its own. Many heard, then read and pondered and preached.

As for Yahweh, Isaiah insists time and again that God is not neutral, unaffected, or self-distanced. God is justice. God has chosen and rejected, taken sides for and against. Chosen are the poor, the remnant, the *anawim*. Conversely, denounced and renounced are the purveyors of injustice whose possessions are a curse, whose look is lethal.

There is small consolation here. The word is no sooner spoken than contravention, anger, retaliation follow. A golden word evokes a hollow or a mocking echo. A fist strikes the mouth of the servant. There is no pause, no mulling or weighing of the word by the adversary, no attempt at accommodation, no second thoughts on the part of these strenuous opponents. Is there no disposition for the truth, no debate or inquiry? None of these is indicated. Is the word of God so inflammatory that persecution is immediate and inevitable?

It is as though the world has made its decision beforehand. According to the oracle, there is no pause, no interval. Is this word not worth granting a hearing, reflection? May it not mysteriously be to the advantage of those who are addressed?

Perhaps, in fact, now and again some consideration is given to the word. (We know that such does happen.) But Isaiah is not concerned with the steps of accommodation or possible acceptance, whatever their purport.

Let us say that God allows Isaiah no space, whether for a word that befits or a world that accepts. He foreshortens and concentrates matters terribly. For our instruction and for our realistic hope as well, the Isaian scenario is sharp, painful, to the point, even appalling. The word of God is spoken. Then follows persecution of the one who dares utter the word.

How out of character is this sternness! We have heard Isaiah, the tenderest, most human of prophets, poet supreme, lover of creation, singer of the song of nonviolence, of return and reconciliation—then this! He whets the blade of God's word to a very razor's edge. Is he holding the blade to our throat?

Does the servant here purvey a kind of preconception, an obsession with failure or, at the least, an unwarrantedly pessimistic view of grace and its persuasive powers? Must the word of God beat and beat at the gate of the world and be refused all access?

For the world's part, is it forever to be stuck, deaf by genetic, malignant choice, deprived of all access to the truth?

Maybe we are too abstract, speaking of the world, when Isaiah is concrete and specific and offers instances. Maybe we should speak rather of those who wield authority in a certain way, those in whose vested interest it is that political, social, military, religious, economic realities not budge off their base. Such have the law in their favor (the law as commonly purveyed being a more or less sophisticated form of seizing and entitling, excluding and punishing—that is, the law of the jungle).

The guardians wield the law as though it were a club, fervently. It is clear, for example, that in cases involving the Plowshares nuclear resisters, judges decide cases before any evidence is heard. Indeed, the relevant evidence is consistently forbidden, put out of sight and mind, deemed irrelevant. In effect, the judge sits with and sides with the prosecution.

Nothing, no one, no call to conscience, no summoning of experts has been able to break through this adamantine wall. The truth strikes, all in vain, and falls to ground. There remains only the legal charade—the charge to the jury, transfixing, boxing them into a predetermined definition of crime and punishment. It is as though jurors must be lobotomized, mutilated in their noblest parts, cleansed of any trace of discernment. Of course, they produce on demand the guilty verdict.

In sum, the text of the legal farce, at once heartless and hilarious, is written beforehand, memorized and huckstered by the parties in power. As far as the defendants are concerned, their world from henceforth will be miniscule indeed. First the dock, then the prison.

In fact, the defendants stand in the dock with the suffering servant. Each is condemned without a hearing. In Isaiah's terse phrases, experience is thus disturbingly syncopated—and, in our experience, disheartingly repeated. His tale is nonetheless true for being so dramatically put.

The servant stands at an impasse; it is a source of deep sorrow. She is sent to all, to those of the household and to the nations. And she is rejected.

Not all reject her, certainly. But there are those who, taking a stand within the law or under cover of law, set about to stifle the word of truth. Further, they degrade and humiliate the servant, reduce her to the suspect status of defendant, a burden of presumed guilt upon her shoulders.

There is a strong implication here as to who is responsible for this charade. Centuries later, in the trial endured by Christ, the implication yields to certainty. The point hinted at in Isaiah is, on occasion of the later travail, made hideously explicit. The powers of this world are revealed as sworn enemies of the truth—and of the truth tellers.

The guardians of the systems of this world sense the presence of the truth—its content, its judgment, its explosive power. They have a kind of sixth sense of the stature of this adversary. So they move against the servant.

The word of truth simply cannot be borne, cannot coexist. It cuts too deep, to the juncture of bone and spirit. Its power is that it unmasks and derogates the pretensions of the last word, the last word which is the feral claim of death.

Thus the word threatens; it offers something more damaging and dangerous than an intellectual critique of systems, good, bad, or indifferent. It is a summons; the systems are hailed to judgment. Again and again, the word declares them illegitimate. It condemns their works and pomp. It opens the prison doors, it judges the savagery of death rows. It judges the judges, them perhaps most sternly of all. It releases and rehabilitates the bondsmen and women, the resisters and sanctuary workers, the market slaves and stoop workers and migrants and illegal aliens.

Can the word redeem also the high and mighty?

Yes, it offers them, too, chained as they are to their thrones and high places, a prospect, an out—freedom.

The word of truth insists that another game be undertaken if humans are to recover their humanity, another game than winners and losers, rich and poor, powerful and powerless. The word summons nonpersons, those condemned and those who condemn, to a dignity, whether lost or spurned or denied.

In so doing, it rejoices in setting worldly matters on their head. It calls an assize, a people's court, puts the persecutors and judges in the dock for their crimes against the humanity of God. This is the toppling of systems that Mary celebrates, like a gentle indomitable fury (Luke 1:46–55).

The imagery of verse 6 summons up not Pilate, shrugging, washing hands, posing idle questions, but Caiaphas or perhaps the mob (or, in another time, a Mississippi sheriff, judge, lynch posse). It speaks of all those for whom the words of the servant, even her presence, what she stands for, are an affront, a stigma, a stain on the mask of purported decency and strict order.

Isaiah or Christ or Martin Luther King or the numerous Plowshares prisoners stand, hands bound, answering nothing to the absurd fabrication of charges. They offer a reproof even in silence, even in custody. For those who are thus castigated, only the removal of the servants from public gaze, from the streets, from utterance, even from the earth itself, can bring a peace of sorts. For the sake of law and order, take them away!

The servant has become the resister and, according to our oracle, she is to be severely tested—physically, psychically, beaten, spat upon, degraded. To think of the servant is to recall Stephen Biko, and so many thousands of others—the disappeared, the tortured of every time and place and especially of our own. For such innocents, the so-called legal process has broken down. It functions, in sane eyes, as the cruelest of jokes. Nearer the point, it was never really applied.

Carnivorous, violent as the system is (the system called justice), it can never be made to function smoothly (even according to its own debased rules of dog-eat-dog, better in packs than one on one) when bearing down on conscientious spirits. In our lifetime, those in charge of the system know that against such spirits "there is no law" (see Gal. 5:23). Liars, false witnesses, judges and prosecutors, squalid and glib and tedious by turn, stand self-revealed. This is the "unmasking" of the powers, of which Dr. King spoke.

In verses 6 and 7 the nonviolence, the indomitability of the accused, standing and withstanding, is described as a form of God's own strength. And rightly so. Not to answer in kind, to retain peace of spirit in the midst of bloody provocation—these wonders are wrought by the power of the Spirit of God. Verse 7 offers the logic quite explicitly: "Yahweh hastens to my side." We will never know fully (even though we know in part) the light that was struck at the death of our martyrs—Stephen Biko, Oscar Romero, Martin Luther King, the women and peasants and catechists and Jesuits of Salvador. We know enough. The consistency, the fervor with which they lived and labored are hint enough of the light, its quality and intensity.

"My will adamant, my soul never confounded." Here we have the image of a steadfast soul. There is no confusion of spirit.

One ponders the words (not as though one were living by them—who could so claim?) to help the words come true against all odds.

These words hardly bespeak average strengths. One invokes them, a kind of mantra, a chant, a hymn in the fiery furnace. Through the words, one implores the strength of that "cloud of witnesses" (see Heb. 12:1) who first uttered them, lived and died by them. How freighted such words are with the greatness of our history. They are the words of martyrs, not, to be sure, words of supermen and women, but of those who simply, and under the harshest duress, kept the faith.

Verses 8 and 9 suggest a trial scene. God sits as judge, or perhaps as jury. It seems that this trial scene stands outside time; it is more in the nature of a last judgment.

In this world, such a scene can take place only in the heart of the accused who knows beyond doubt that he is innocent, and that he will be vindicated (but not here, not now.) In this world the accused will be found guilty. That is the ironbound law of the Fall, which claims for its own a chief principality, the system of so-called justice.

The servant stands there, not only as the accused, but as already convicted and criminalized. Yet God has gone further even; God stands with the criminal Christ. Thus the faith of Isaiah penetrates the sordid temporal courtroom and declares an outcome that can only be termed audacious. According to the unshakable faith of the prophet, an altogether predictable outcome is turned on its head.

The drama gets underway, but the denouement, strange to say, is announced beforehand. What a literal bold faith!

A dare is issued. Let the accuser (prosecutor) stand forth. Let him face me. Let us together weigh the evidence, weigh our chances, his and mine. (In Revelation, the prosecutor is identified as Satan; the "one who accuses the just, night and day" [12:10]).

"With God standing by me, who will condemn me? Whoever (attempts it) will fall away to rags, like a garment. The moths will consume them" (50:9). Commonly, prosecutors present themselves as spiffy types; judges are robed in dignity and decorum. "Hizzoner enters, minions in his wake! All rise!"

According to Isaiah, this pretension, this pinch-penny grandeur must be peeled away, decontaminated, demythologized, in order that the truth may appear, the truth that ritual and decor serve so straitly to banish.

Then indeed comes an epiphany. The truth enters when through another door comes the accused. Then and now, it is the prisoner whose gaze sees through it all—his contemned estate, the suspicion and indifference of the curious and frivolous, the uncertainty of the weak, their veiled terror, the lubricious self-congratulation of his persecutors. Permeating all with a faint stench is the atmosphere of an abattoir of the spirit, a place where justice eons ago was hanged, drawn, quartered, and buried (at the time, say, when Cain slew his brother). These grant the accused a wonderful concentration of mind. He looks around him. His third eye is open.

The accusers are regarded with a large measure of contempt; they appear as images of death and diminishment. Their garments speak for them: greatness, import, ego, sovereignty, the last word—deterrence, the power of life and death. What is there of human substance, compassion, wisdom, or truthfulness? There is not much—more exactly, nothing. It is as though the garments were empty; they are draped about hollow disembodied ghosts. The robes fall away to rags, and the moths flock to the feast.

The truth is made evident at last. The garments were a sign, signifying nothing; they were the cerements of corpses. They were wired for sound; zombies spoke through them. The dead spoke—only of death, death as a social method of dealing with human grievances. Dispose of the living and presto! the problem vanishes.

Christians are commonly instructed from their youth to be great respecters of the law. This admonition would seem to separate us from Isaiah and other great spirits in rather startling fashion. Early on, a far different attitude marked our ancestors in the faith. First came the Pauline assault on the law as savior, then the diatribe of the apostle James against judges. The courts, it appeared, were declared off limits to litigious Christians, whatever the offense for which they sought reparation. Along with the military, courts represented an assault on the sovereignty of God who said, "Justice is mine."

Later generations, for various complicated reasons, fled once more to the shelter of law. It was a rude shack indeed, hardly standing in place! In the ensuing centuries, Christians paid large tribute of idolatry to the law of the land. The law of this or that nation state (it mattered little which one, how virtuous or criminal) was once more reinstated as savior.

By and large, Christians consider themselves justified by keeping the law. Thus a monstrous antisavior, the savior of property, investment, civil order, national security, the savior-armies, "lurches toward Bethlehem to be born."

The image endures; so does the reality. The beast is perennially born anew, seizing on ever new and persuasive forms, now brutal, now subtle. Yet this beast is always assured of Christian bed, board, and welcome, not in the outer shed or stable, but in the front parlor!

He thrives, he battens, he justifies, condemns, he makes a wreckage of landscape and heart. "The end of the world," Thomas Merton wrote, "will be legal." Until we understand that, we have underestimated the pernicious force of the law, hailed by the nuclear powers into the justifying of the Final Omnicrime.

In the final analysis, Isaiah, and we, are instructed to seek justice only from God.

My Just One: Seized, Convicted, Punished
(52:13–15; 53:1–12)
The Fourth Song of the Servant of Yahweh

My servant!
a victim
borne to the abattoir,
a plant languishing
in sterile ground

in guise scarcely human,
no dignity, no beauty—
despised, rejected,
beneath notice utterly.

Snatched from among the living
condemned by sinners—
who worked this infamy?

Dissembling, desperate,
clamorous with;
       Ave Caesar!
It was for us, the lost,
for us she suffered.

But see—
an Easter dawn,

a flood of light!
the world to come
at long last, come!

(In the oracle adapted above, I have followed, perhaps too
freely, the suggestions of the Jerusalem Bible, to wit and in general:
  • persecution and patience, 53:7
  • the scandalizing of petty "believers," 52:14–15
  • suffering as expiation and intercession, 53:4, 6, 8, 10–12. The

servant will triumph, and will be crowned as faithful one, 53:10–12.)

The translation of Isaiah 52:13—53:12 of *The New Jerusalem Bible* is given here for convenience:

52:13   Look, my servant will prosper,
           will grow great, will rise to great heights.

    14   As many people were aghast at him
           —he was so inhumanly disfigured
           that he no longer looked like a man—

    15   so many nations will be astonished
           and kings will stay tight-lipped before him,
           seeing what had never been told them,
           learning what they had not heard before.

53:1   Who has given credence to what we have heard?
           And who has seen in it a revelation of Yahweh's arm?

    2   Like a sapling he grew up before him,
           like a root in arid ground.
           He had no form or charm to attract us,
           no beauty to win our hearts;

    3   he was despised, the lowest form of men,
           a man of sorrows, familiar with suffering,
           one for whom, as it were, we averted our gaze,
           despised, for whom we had no regard.

    4   Yet ours were the sufferings he was bearing,
           ours the sorrows he was carrying,
           while we thought of him as someone being punished
           and struck with affliction by God;

    5   whereas he was being wounded for our rebellions,
           crushed because of our guilt;
           the punishment reconciling us fell on him,
           and we have been healed by his bruises.

    6   We had all gone astray like sheep,
           each taking his own way,
           and Yahweh brought the acts of rebellion
           of all of us to bear on him.

    7   Ill-treated and afflicted,
           he never opened his mouth,

> like a lamb led to the slaughter-house,
> like a sheep dumb before its shearers
> he never opened his mouth.

8 Forcibly, after sentence, he was taken.
   Which of his contemporaries was concerned
   at his having been cut off from the land of the living,
   at his having been struck dead for his people's rebellion?
9 He was given a grave with the wicked,
   and his tomb is with the rich,
   although he had done no violence,
   had spoken no deceit.

10 It was Yahweh's good pleasure to crush him with pain;
   if he gives his life as a sin offering,
   he will see his offspring and prolong his life,
   and through him Yahweh's good pleasure will be done.

11 After the ordeal he has endured,
   he will see the light and be content.
   By his knowledge, the upright one, my servant will justify
       many
   by taking their guilt on himself.

12 Hence I shall give him a portion with the many,
   and he will share the booty with the mighty,
   for having exposed himself to death
   and for being counted as one of the rebellious,
   whereas he was bearing the sin of many
   and interceding for the rebellious.

This final song of the servant is replete with suffering but ends with abrupt vindication. Yet many difficulties, a multitude of them, hem in the figure of the mysterious servant as well as the nature and source of her suffering. Further, we have, so to speak, no second opinion at hand. No other prophet takes up the theme of the servant. By way of contrast, each of the four evangelists offers a nuance, flavor, emphasis, as to the character, deeds, and, at times, the firsthand words of one and the same Christ. Yet this servant never once speaks for herself.

We are told various things about her, unidentified as she is. She will endure extraordinary suffering with patience. She will undergo (perhaps most difficult of all) the scandal of the pusillanimous, those who at one time placed a certain trust, immature and tentative to be sure, in her and her vocation. They are somewhat like Job's friends, concluding with an aura of covert self-satisfaction that he must be cursed of God, since awful things befall him. We learn, moreover, that the sufferings of the servant are a form of intercession on behalf of others. Finally, we are assured that the servant will be vindicated, though too late to save her life, a cold comfort at best.

Thus the oracle unfolds as though on two or three stages, one above the other. First, God speaks briefly (52:13–15). Then the form of the song is clarified; it is partly (though in small part) a biography. The life of the servant is told, always as though from above or outside (53:1–10). The narrators are a diverse mix, in one way or another involved in the events. Finally, God sums up (53:11–12). God's words put a brake to the rather more theological lucubrations of the other speakers.

Who, we might be inclined to ask, speaks for the mysterious protagonist, the one who by presumption (better, fiction) of the author, cannot speak for herself? This one is described or analyzed or damned with faint praise, or overpraised, but never once is heard from.

At what point and by whom, in other words, is the truth of God's word being conveyed to us? Are possible literary devices at work, hyperbole, irony? Are we to believe that the speakers, taking the role of a king and a chorus of citizens, offer a truthful version of the servant? Are various ideologies and special interests involved? Are the speakers to be heard with a wary ear, illustrating as they do a coverup, guilt posing sympathy?

The king takes up a variety of themes—reproach, astonishment, admiration, regret (and implied moral confusion). He is joined, it would seem, by a kind of Greek chorus of the citizens, commenting on the action. All admit, here and there, to a measure of guilt with regard to the servant's plight. But the guilt, whose cause is identified, floats free and undefined on the air. No crime is specified. Did many, in fact, have part in crimes against the innocent one? We are not told. We face a dense thicket of difficulties indeed!

At the start (52:13–15), a measure of incoherence prevails. God introduces the servant, taking a justified pride in the moral stature of the chosen one.

But greatness proves pitifully vulnerable and is shortly undercut. The admirable servant is marked for destruction. Those who had venerated her and hearkened to her word are appalled. They rush to and fro, as in a surreal blur of panic at the condition of this virtuous one brought low. What can have happened? Implied is the question of who brought this to pass. The kings of earth are onlookers, perhaps more. In any case, there is no hint of responsibility or guilt at this point, only vexations, Kafkaesque darkness. The kings, authorities unidentified, the people—someone, some awful faceless power, brought the servant low!

Probably the fiasco was wrought through legal means (53:8), which may be a clue as to why we are kept in the dark. Was it simply taken for granted that the trial, those who orchestrated it, as well as those in attendance who kept silent, were above board? If so, we have an ironic "transhistorical" hint, that is, it was ever thus, and thus it shall be.

At the beginning of things all is rosy, favorable to the servant. Indeed, God's eye is on the servant, the apple of the divine gaze: "High, prosperous, lifted up, greatly exalted. . . ." Yet the words have a kind of desperate hopeful ring, an aura of "despite all," or "it shall be at the end of things," or, "let them wreak their worst, I will have the last word" (but meantime, few or no words at all!).

This life includes, we learn, a surfeit of innocent suffering, and no one is held accountable—literally no one. Neither kings nor judges nor prosecutors nor the multitudes of this world are named as guilty. The latter, it seems, are always present but remain morally shadowy, by turns pious, loquacious and self-serving, great wringers and washers of hands, but never, Isaiah hints, held accountable.

The world and its powers cannot comprehend the behavior of the innocent one, showing persistence in the face of wounding and an unassailable, even scornful silence. The blank inability of the persecutors (prosecutors?) to break through, break him down, is a hint as to the source of the astonishment of the multitude, as well as of the set jaw of the rulers. The world has no moral equipment to grasp moral greatness, let alone to emulate it. All are stalemated, baffled, infuriated, and, to that extent, more determined, more dangerous to the Holy One.

It is hard not to take much of the proceedings for a front. The drama is played out in public. A deconstruction of the scene and its words might go along these lines:

> Our position is this; we know nothing. We came on the scene after the fact so to speak. We had no part in this admitted outrage. And in any case, the victim has been of small help to legitimate authorities; his choice to remain silent, in a sense, ties our hands.

Those who look on are amazed at what they see—the behavior, the silence laced with scorn, the great refusal of such a one as the servant become the defendant. Is it collusion or collision—or perhaps both? The crowds have known only themselves and those who rule them. The authorities have known only one another and the crowds. Rulers and crowds, each labored under a huge misconception that the functioning of a just society vindicated their usages.

Ignored in all this was something known in the world as simple cowardice, the silence that kills. To our actors this implied no moral lapse at all, but a prudence required of those who walk to the drumbeat of law, order, and the skirmishings of power.

This willed ignorance, a kind of protective cover, exhausted new possibilities and crushed alternatives. In all the world, there were only those in charge, those who buckled under, those who gave orders, and those who marched to the whip. Such, one reflects, is the imperial message to its citizens and to the world at large. In time, the message takes on the force of a metaphysical principle— in this and no other way is the world constituted.

Not to be missed is the imperative, the threat implied; any deviants from the norm will be required to pay up. Therefore, prudence keeps a discreet mouth and eye and ear; see no evil, hear no evil. . . .

This servant appeared out of nowhere, as far as can be learned, out of no predictable genetic line. Her existence, her moral stature, come as shock; she seems a sole member of an unknown species. She is by no means a slave. Slaves can be dealt with. Servants cannot, at least servants like this one who is servant of Yahweh and of no other in creation. Here is a servant, gifted or cursed or both, with a conscience unviolated and, as shortly is to be manifest, a conscience inviolate.

The tragedy that lurks around the servant like a coven of Eumenides awaiting its moment can be understood only if the servant and the kings and the crowds, in harmony and conflict, are attentively considered. Who circles about whom, who is at center, who holds legitimacy, who kowtows, who is guilty (and of what) and who innocent?

In the midst of all, towering above all, both withholding and lending mystery and depth and meaning, silent as an empty grave, stands the great Refuser. The servant of Yahweh remains, in the Buddhist way, mindful, attentive, with the concentration only suffering may be thought to confer. Intractable, she dares even in silence to raise questions.

Who questions authority, then or now? The kings are corrupt, the people a flock of mindless sheep. Questions are ill received by the edgy authorities and their undifferentiated lackeys and victims, the crowd of loyal citizens. Questions certainly imply a threat to the powers of this world, a threat but also a hope—perhaps for many, an only hope.

The Jerusalem Bible takes 53:1 as a direct quotation from the mouths of rulers and people. If so, we have a kind of pious dodge, "Who could believe what God has wrought?" Such a tendency is by no means rare. One raises one's eyes to heaven in stupefaction of spirit, in face of human misfortune (in which one has played a role, large or small), and thus deflects attention from the aforesaid complicities.

The people or the kings continue to describe their connection with the servant (53:2–3). Has familiarity bred contempt? "We had every reason to believe we knew this one. . . ." Worth noting is their chosen role of more or less guilty bystanders. They distance themselves, and we look in vain for an index of responsibility. They are like late arrivals at a scene of carnage, too late to prevent the tragedy (or so they would have us believe). An atmosphere of more or less detached sympathy prevails. It is all quite surreal—and less than convincing.

Several questions, quite naturally arising in the circumstance, are never dealt with. Presupposing that "we have seen him thus, how did his fearsome condition arise? Should we not even now investigate, and issue a report, even if such should implicate ourselves?"

Short of such honorable search, does not a suspicion come to rest on the bystanders, or is the destruction of the servant to be considered only a kind of disaster in nature, a blind fate?

The servant, be it noted once more, never speaks for herself. Why this persistent silence? We are granted no hint. Of the meaning of the silence of Jesus before Herod and Pilate, a mitigated silence to be sure, we have the broadest hints, and more. Here, not a word is uttered. The nameless servant stands there, silent as the unborn, the silence passive, impassive. She is spoken about by others, like a child or a mental deficient or a mute or like someone already dead. In this last instance, the story of the servant's life and death is at the disposition of others, merciful, savory, manipulative, self-indulgent as they may be. Will a cult arise, or will the dead be twice buried in the amnesia of the living?

The people cover their faces as before a leper (53:3). This is both a ritual and a psychological response. The sight is too much, the smell too much. One thinks of leprosy and the law, also of the usual reaction today, to those ill with AIDS.

The people seem, after the fact, chastened in spirit (53:4). The image recalls another scene in a later century. A band of disciples were clotted together for dazed comfort after the passion and death of Christ. They were cowed in spirit, broken in heart, knowing that through betrayal and denial and cowardice their part in his death was large.

As for Isaiah's heroic protagonist, for all the horror of the scene, the machinations of authorities and the crowd, something hopeful is underway. The victim holds firm; perhaps through her those responsible are being cleansed of illusions.

"It was for us, the lost, for us she suffered" (see 53:5 and 6). The servant is granted no chance to explain, to vindicate motives, to assert herself as human. Interpreting the tragic fate of the servant is a tricky and troubling affair. We must tread lightly. The expiation theme may be far afield from the servant's self-understanding. When, toward the end, God speaks, we have a much more immediate and modest interpretation.

Drawing analogies with the Christ story, one could treat the death of the Savior as compounded with one's own time and place, in the deaths of martyrs and innocents. In consequence of this insight, one might feel urged to shoulder a portion of the burden of life, vocation, fidelity, rather than thrusting these on others.

Also, with regard to the suffering of the innocent, it seems better not to reach too easily for a religious explanation. A double, concatenated reality might then emerge, as Paul suggests. "Christ, having suffered once and for all," is balanced by our "making up in our bodies what is lacking in his passion" (see Col. 1:24). Yet we are well advised also to make no great claims for ourselves in such matters as endurance, heroism, and the rest, as though we were expiating the "sins of others." This claim is insulting and can only becloud sane understanding.

Even so, is it not true that the sufferings of the innocent avail on behalf of others, ourselves in fact? The Scripture includes such declarations. A vivid sense of complicity in sin is laudable and of God. We have had enough of scapegoating. A sense of solidarity in sin is worthy as long as such leads us to action on behalf of others, those who are viewed as our equals, at the least, and more realistically, as our moral betters.

A servant song, it would seem, ought at some point, to celebrate the changes wrought in us through the example and words of the holy one. In this sense, the verses under discussion seem preliminary. To the degree that they speak of sin and repentance but not of consequent moral behavior, they are to be considered incomplete. They raise an iconic hero, a Christlike figure before us, but they neglect to commend the task implied—our taking up the cross of the times. Thus the song invites thoughtfulness. Who are we, and where do we stand in the noble line of the holy ones? What are we to do with our lives?

One cannot but think of the healing offered the North American church though the atrocious sufferings of sisters and brothers in the Central and Latin American church. This is to be accounted a peerless gift. We are led gratefully and humbly to contrast present attitudes and acts of resistance with the silence that marked and marred the churches during the Vietnam war. There was no thunderous "No!" from most quarters, pulpits or chanceries, not a word, for years and years. The ideal servant, here under harsh duress, invites us servants to speak up, risk, put life to the test.

The text emphasizes the silence of the servant before the accusers in court. In contrast, conscientious defendants in the courts of America habitually open their mouths, vociferously, in the course of their trials and confinements. They regard this speaking up as part of the responsibility that led them, in the first instance, to violate unjust laws. Subsequently they must tell why. Sane politics and spirituality demand it.

Perhaps there is no great contrast here. We remember how Christ played it both ways. In the course of his trial, at times he held his peace in face of the frivolous or overweening. And again he spoke up, loud and clear.

The illegitimate or intemperate questioning by judges and prosecutors, their hectoring, bickering, mocking, provoking of defendants are rightly met with silence, a silence that spells scorn. But when the truth can be conveyed, or evidence of good faith is shown (how rarely!), or when the larger public can be addressed (the media being largely ignorant or indifferent), then we are well advised to speak up.

Perhaps a deeper meaning is implied here—the will to stand by one's actions, come hell or prison or death itself. At peace with one's conduct, and in full view of consequences, one pays up.

The part played by God in the wicked proceedings is heavily underscored (see 53:4, 6, 10). Again, we proceed with caution. One does not lightly set out to walk through such deep waters.

The doctrine of expiation is proposed by the people and the authorities, by those, in other words, whose own interests are at stake, who have most to gain by attributing a religious meaning to the events. Thereby they pass the buck.

Yet the question persists, What part did the crowd, the judges, the prosecutors, the kings, play in the scene? Were there not scenes behind the scene, dodges and ploys "in chambers," bargains struck, bribes passed, any and all of these aimed at the destruction of the just one? These authorities are hardly to be thought the most disinterested witnesses or reporters.

Beginning with verse 4, the speakers vent a strange language, admiring, enumerating emotionally, all but groveling.

Lengthy references are made to "our sufferings (she bore), . . . our sorrows (she carried)," and then, more strikingly, "we thought of her as chastised, stricken, humiliated . . . pierced for our sins . . . crushed because of our crimes. . . . God made our iniquity fall on her. . . . For our sins, she was stricken with death." These sentiments might be thought a kind of sanctimonious hectoring of the servant.

Two interpretations suggest themselves. First, we have here a report of events followed by a theological interpretation—the expiatory sacrifice of the servant. By supposition these are to be taken at face value: This is what happened, and this is what biblical folk accept concerning what happened. The speakers, according to this version, are a literary device. They stand surrogate for Isaiah in conveying event and meaning.

An alternative is that we are offered an account that exempts the reporters from all responsibility. Their hands are tied; their task is merely to record events, and so they remain determinedly "objective" in face of the trial, condemnation, and death. In this hypothesis, the report is followed by a theological cover-up. We, authorities and people, were the more or less horrified witnesses of events. We were helpless to intervene. For God decreed all this, or at least allowed it to happen, in order to bring good out of manifest evil.

Indeed, the speakers are, in more senses than one, extremely shadowy figures.

One notes, too, that the theme of guilt is treated almost offhandedly. It is admitted that "we went our own way, we sinned, and the like." But the errancy, the sin, is kept (more or less deliberately) vague. No details are offered. This, one thinks, is a religion of indifference, of moral neutrality. The atmosphere seems strangely redolent of speculative theology, or a conventional, all but casual liturgy.

No finger points, least of all at the speakers. No specific crime is adduced, no guilty party indicted. But is no one guilty? Was not a crime committed, under the guise of a so-called justice system, against the just one? Was not this a kangaroo court? Were not the trial and judgment and execution a cruel farce?

One longs to ask: Who was responsible for the supposed legal proceeding, for the capital sentence? Do facts point to the speakers or to others unnamed? Why are we told nothing of such crucial matters?

The dictum that God brings good out of evil is, of course, theologically impeccable. The trouble starts when the dictum is hauled forward as a cover. We might imagine the chorus of prior speakers explaining:

> The servant, admirable as she may be, got in the way of things as they are. Intemperate talk was followed by tumult among the people. Consequences followed swiftly; punishment came down hard, perhaps too hard. It must even be admitted that in the heat of the occasion, a measure of justice went awry.
>
> Surely, we regret the lapse. But of course we were only onlookers, bystanders. And now that the dust has settled, we remain both grateful and edified. The holy defendant has taken the harsh proceedings so well, meek and humble and wordless, a sheep to the slaughter, just as the Bible commends.

The chorus of pieties reach a climax in verse 10. Talk about Job's comforters, or the wicked burying the just! "God was pleased to crush (the servant) through suffering. She will receive length of days. And things pleasing to God will be accomplished through her." Like Job's theologically inclined friends, these worthies are so sure of themselves! so sure about God!

This mealy-mouthed implication is not to be pursued, let alone approved. God offers a far different version of events; it might be thought to go like this:

> Must I not weep to tell it? I summoned my servant as witness to truth and justice. And she responded, in season and out, whether in fear or fearlessness.
>
> Then came the awful outcome, inevitable it would seem from the start, given the world, a darkness I myself only partially penetrate.
>
> My servant's words and acts, that ABC of godliness I taught her—love of the poor, reproaches toward the rich, trust though

weakness entail—these were badly received by the worldly principalities. She was plucked away, forced through the knothole of the legal system. And predictably—but you know the rest, you the bystanders, you the powerful.

She was faithful to the end. And I swear, through her, you will yet see great things come to pass.

In the text when God speaks up (53:11–12), there is a notable modesty in the words, terse statements of praise for the life and death of the servant. The dogma of expiation, so dear to the kings and citizens, is entirely ignored. The inspiration and example of the servant are praised: "After the testing of her soul, she will see the light and be consoled."

Indeed, darkness surrounded the last days of the servant. She must often have wondered in a torpor of grief and loss whether the sun had vanished from the sky, a common enough feeling among those enduring the rigors of law.

In such lives, conscious innocence is by no means consoling; it is no more than another point of anguish. The question that comes home like a stiletto is not, "Why do the innocent suffer?" but "Why do I, who am innocent, suffer?"

In this situation, God who is by self-definition Light, is become darkness.

What is to be said of a providence that withholds all providing—all caring, cherishing of one who is by every right, "more than lilies of the field or birds of the air"?

Whatever light and consolation might be thought to exist are all but quenched. Little or nothing of either is available, at least for such as the servant—or for such as Christ, as we learn from the cry that shatters the air of Calvary.

These are matters to be accepted with an edgy yes, a monosyllable sometimes grudging, seldom fullhearted. We call it faith. The servant, like most of her kind, sees little come of the life to which she was called. God is silent, silent as the grave her persecutors are fervently choosing, digging, cordoning off. Theirs is the self-appointed task, no less pressing, of destroying not only the servant's good name but also her sense of ever having possessed one.

"By her sufferings [not 'by his knowledge'], my servant will bring many to justice, even as she bears their iniquities" (53:11) The iniquities, as is not often pointed out, are precisely the injustice that brings suffering to the servant. It is tempting to underscore the irony here. The servant has been denied justice in this world, and she brings others to justice. This is not, be it noted, the bar of worldly justice. She has finished with that (as it has finished her). The servant's example and grace go deeper. She invites the unjustified to the justice of God, that is to say, to holiness, to the all but unimaginable possibility of love.

Included in the ample scope of her love are those who presumed to speak for her, and in so doing, gagged her mouth. The interlocutors, the crowd, the authorities, those in whose interest it was to issue theological pronunciamentos, uttered a very lava flow of pseudo-wisdom interpreting (misinterpreting) the servant's behavior. Also those same worthies, perhaps, skillfully dodged their part in her death. Included also are the generations to come—the pseudo-biographers, hagiographers, and pious distorters of truth—anxious to "clean up the act."

Power now flows from the once powerless one. Verse 12 calls to mind the "great hinge" of Paul's letter to the Philippians, "Because Christ was obedient even unto death, therefore God exalted him and conferred on him a name above every name. . ." (2:8–9).

Thus, early on, a kind of principled understanding is struck between God and the servant. No blank checks descend, fluttering from on high. No promises are made of vindication, glory, good times, happy outcomes.

Providence? All one sees is a dark cloud. The hideous process of this world, the destruction of the innocent, proceeds on schedule. It is as though God does not exist, or has simply given up on humankind, vanished from the world, as once, according to Ezekiel, in scorn and rejection the Glory departed from the Jerusalem temple.

The servant, deprived of any protector, may be considered and dealt with as a criminal, for all the world knows or cares (recalling the murder of women, children, Jesuits, Romero, and countless others, with no voice from the church denouncing the crimes, and the executioners sensing their immunity, and proceeding). The crime is interference, the crying out in a lucid voice, speaking of forbidden themes.

So the servant stands in the dock, alongside the social jetsam washed up with the awesome rhythm of a high tide. She guards her soul, her self-respect. She is hard as adamant, not to be corrupted or swayed. She is tried under the same laws as apply to crimes of small or big losers.

The laws are promulgated in the main to keep certain properties inviolable, off limits, sacred even, including the most hideous illegitimate properties, properties that rightly understood are larcenies against the poor. And worse, these properties are tokens of the will to engage in mass murder—nuclear properties.

The servant will not be vindicated in this world, we are told. Still, the effect of such a life one day will be known. Multitudes will hear and see; tributes will be placed at her tomb.

Thus, the vindication of the just need not rest on a theory of expiation of others' sins in order to be found precious in the eyes of the Lord. Indeed, the death of the just is of great and solemn weight; it cannot fail to affect others to come, in perpetuum.

The servant has sought no justification. Her appeal has been to God only. She pleads neither works nor orthodoxy nor discipline nor cultural approval nor the nod of the great nor, finally, that court of last appeal, an appeal utterly futile: justification by the law.

In austerity and carefulness of spirit, the servant beckons others to seek the source of all justification—the source of existence itself, of meaning, of capacity for love, received and given.

There was no choice between dying or not dying, the common fate. There was a choice only about the manner and circumstance of dying. One could fade out, vanish with a shrug and a murmur of "things as they are," the low profile of the cowed and coward. Or, one could deck out one's soul in the tawdry robe of the "justice system," hum along, echo the cliches, lock step in a moral crepuscule.

The servant seeks a third way. She offers a paradigm; we are to make of it what we will. Seek justice all the days of one's life—and take the heat, the consequences. Thus she beckons others toward the same freedom she evidenced in the noble proffer of her life.

Thus, too, her example is multiplied like bread—friends, servants, sisters, brothers, abroad, at home. Her story is at hand for those who seek, one and the same gesture of soul: Come, this is the way!

Christ, so often identified with the protagonist of Isaiah, bore in his flesh, we are told, the sins of many. He bore in his flesh the sins of Pilate, Herod, Caiaphas, the executioners, soldiers, police, the people. He bore as well the sins of recusant disciples, the sins of family members who early on concluded he was mad and washed hands of him.

One can indeed enlarge the scope, understanding that such crimes are endemic to every place and time, crimes against the just. We are called to cry out against such crimes, which generally go unchallenged, in church and out. Such sins in the old catechism were described as "crying to heaven for vengeance."

Finally, the servant "intercedes for the transgressors." The image is of a kind of advocate, an attorney of defense. Imagine! Prosecuted to the fullest rigor of the law, denounced by apoplectic property holders, chimeric priests, sloths in the guise of sages—disposed of, put to death, the servant possesses her soul. Yet her life and death have been an intercession on behalf of criminal authority.

It does not do justice to the moral greatness of the servant to say she did not respond in kind. She went further, a long, long way further. To say that her conduct became in effect, the only hope of the unjust is a large claim indeed. But it is accurate in describing the understanding of those who confront the law on issues like war, civil or human rights, or sanctuary protest.

The reversal of fortune is staggering. The defendants are stripped of recourse, their work vilified, their good name held to scorn. When all seems lost, when all is in fact lost, their fate is transfigured. They become the mighty protagonists of a quite different drama, of which the visible one can be called only a tawdry, mocking mimicry.

The prosecutors perform their duty, accusing the just. And the just, in response, invoke the mercy of God on their tormentors, a sweet revenge indeed.

Need it be added that if this momentous reversal is to occur, if prosecutors and executioners are to be transformed, such will come to pass only when God at long last hearkens to the tears of her servants. Meantime, while time lasts, they linger "under the altar, the souls of those who had been killed because they proclaimed God's word and had been faithful in their witnessing. They shouted in a loud voice, 'Almighty Lord, holy and true, how long will it be until you judge the dwellers on the earth. . . ?" (Rev. 6:9–10)

But see—
an Easter dawn,
a flood of light!

the world to come
at long last, come!